Dissent and Descent

Essays on Methodism and Roman Catholicism

edited by

Brian Frost and Leo Pyle

LONDON

EPWORTH PRESS

Enquiries should be addressed to
The Methodist Publishing House
Wellington Road
Wimbledon
London SW19 8EU

SBN 7162 0238 9

Printed in Great Britain by
The Garden City Press Limited,
Letchworth, Hertfordshire SG6 1JS

Dissent and Descent

Contents

Contents

Introduction

FOR SOME YEARS a joint commission of the World Methodist Council and the Roman Catholic Church has been engaged in dialogue on theological questions and social collaboration. The commission was established after the World Methodist Conference in 1966.

On August 23rd, 1971, Cardinal Willebrands, President of the Secretariat for Promoting Christian Unity, addressed the assembly of the World Methodist Council in Denver, U.S.A. He drew attention in his address to points which Roman Catholics and Methodists have in common, especially a strong emphasis on the search for holiness.

This set the seal on a growing feeling among Catholics and Methodists that they have much to share and discover for their mutual enrichment.

The Information Service of the Secretariat for Promoting Christian Unity in *The Vatican City*, number 21, May 1973, included the following observation in its report on the Joint Roman Catholic/Methodist Commission:

What can Roman Catholics and Methodists do together? There have been international conversations between us since 1967; the report was agreed in 1970, and is available in various forms. A summary, now being prepared, will be published shortly, and we hope that it will be widely studied.

The conversations have now been started again, and those who are taking part in them want your support. The work already done shows that we hold a great deal in common both in faith and morals. We should now bear joint witness to these truths in common proclamation and action.

It goes on to ask Roman Catholics and Methodists to consider together questions of leadership and authority, spirituality, old and new, moral questions, salvation today and the agreement on the Eucharist reached by Roman Catholic and Anglican conversations, as well as Methodist participation in Church Union negotiations across the world.

This book, *Dissent and Descent*, gathering together as it does essays by Roman Catholics and Methodists in Britain, is one useful way of the two communions in the United Kingdom meeting this request. The editors hope that it will form the basis for local groups of the two churches to come together for discussion, perhaps throughout Lent, in order to get to know each other more deeply and to consider ways of working out the requests of the joint commission.

The book is an independent attempt by a group of people to consider vital issues which Christians face in modern society and to help two groups to understand more profoundly their living traditions. The first four chapters conclude with questions for a study group to answer, as well as a book list to help those who wish to study these matters further to find relevant material.

BRIAN FROST
LEO PYLE

8

1

CHURCH AND SOCIETY

John Lampard and Monica Lawlor

The Catholic Church in England

MONICA LAWLOR

IN A COMPLEX, industrialized, urban society most people are members of many groups which demand from them diverse roles and modes of behaviour. Within such a society persons whose contacts do not extend beyond the primary group of an encapsulated family or community are, both numerically and socially, unusual and much of the multiple group or sub-group membership experienced by the majority may be a matter of individual preference, a fairly free selection among alternatives. An individual's early social contacts are normally determined by the context of his family, but the neighbourhood in which he lives, the school he attends, the place where he works are all to some extent chosen, although social disadvantage may severely limit the range of choices available or the individual or his family's ability to make use of whatever freedom is his.

In such a complex society it is possible to consider religious affiliation as a chosen option, which imposes upon the individual no greater degree of constraint than membership of the local branch of a political party or membership of a golf club. On the other hand an individual may be a member of a religious minority group for reasons which are entirely beyond his own control: his ethnic origin, the colour of his skin, the beliefs of his parents, the place of his birth, may pre-determine his place in society, the opportunities available to him and the attitudes which other people adopt towards him. To use the term 'minority group' to describe any sub-group can make for confusion; for example, in the United States of America the white Anglo-Saxon Protestant may be in an absolute numerical minority (compared with all other groups taken together), but because of the status value of each of these qualifications he would more commonly be said to belong to an elite sub-group than to a minority group. The term 'minority group' tends to carry with it some connotation of social disadvantage; or, at the very least, some distinction or separateness of identity which marks the group off from the general culture or the accepted cultural norms; while 'sub-group' seems to be a more neutral term. True minority groups are partly maintained by forces external to the group, which may often take the form of prejudice or selective disadvantage, but which range all the way from outright persecution to mild estrangement. At the same time there are powerful internal forces making for identity, conformity and cohesion within the group itself: these may take the form of a fierce determination to resist acculturation, to preserve a valued way of life, or, at a simpler level, a mere tendency towards cohesion as a means of mutual protection.

The general thesis of this essay is that both the sociological and the psychological characteristics of the Roman Catholic[1] communion in England can best be understood by accepting that, historically, the Catholic Church in England has been a minority group and by attempting to see how far it may still be understood in this way.

Groups which are essentially elective in character may have a high degree of mutual permeability; such seems to be the case with the Protestant denominations in the United States. According to Thomas,[2] Protestants may change their denominational affiliation without difficulty, either social or psychological, and inter-marriage in common. By contrast there is little permeability between the Catholic Church and the Protestant Churches generally; inter-marriage is difficult and changes of denomination across this boundary (numerically rather rare) involve extensive social consequences when they are made in either direction. The situation in England is made a little different because of the existence of an established Church from which all other communions in some measure or another 'dissent'. There are, moreover, some social class considerations which could reduce the ready interchange of members between some of the Protestant Churches. In spite of these differences, the real barriers to permeability are broadly the same in England and in the United States, that is they are between the Protestant Churches as a whole and the Roman Catholics and the Jews—both the latter can be considered as true minority groups. With recent immigration, the Muslim have come to be a further distinct religious minority in England, as for very different reasons, they have become a distinguishable minority in the United States.

Both in England and in the United States the Roman Catholic and Jewish groups can be broadly considered as both ethnic and religious minorities, and it is this double identification which seems to be responsible for the minority group status that may be recognized for both groups. Although there are extensive similarities between the situation of English and American Catholics, necessarily there are also differences which limit the extent to which it is possible to draw on United States sources and studies in an attempt to understand the social and psychological situation of English Catholics. Perhaps understandably, American psychologists and sociologists have been the main source of our knowledge of the dynamics both of minority groups themselves and the prejudices which have helped to maintain them. Comparable English studies are both more sparse and essentially derivative.[3]

There are three distinct threads to English Roman Catholicism: there are the descendants of the English recusant families,[4] there are the Irish Catholic immigrants and their descendants and finally there is the small but steady stream of converts to the Catholic faith, many of them Anglican clergymen or intellectuals. The present character of Roman Catholicism in England is largely determined by the forced blending of these elements which took place in the nineteenth century. To understand the present preoccupations of the Catholic Church in England it is necessary to understand what happened in the nineteenth century. The native English Catholics were, by the time of Catholic Emancipation, a very small group made up for the most part of aristocratic recusant Catholic families and the people who lived on their estates or under their protection. At the time of the Oxford Movement a number of extremely distinguished Anglicans joined the Church as converts; the most distinguished of these converts was John Henry Newman, but they were mostly men of ability and distinction whose conversion had an importance quite disproportionate to their actual number. It should perhaps be emphasized that their distinction was intellectual or academic and that they were mostly in Anglican orders; although they were an elite with the exception of a few early aristocratic converts they were not an elite by reason of aristocratic birth, great material wealth, or political power. During the next hundred years the Catholic Church continued to attract a significant number of converts of this calibre. The Church owes an immense debt to these converts since they gave her the only real intellectual life she evinced during that period, and they helped to make her in the long run both respectable and socially acceptable.

However the strongest force which shaped the Church during the same period of time was massive immigration from Ireland—a migration that started with the Irish famines and the building of the railways and continues to this day. In the nineteenth century the bulk of those immigrants were desperately poor, unskilled, manual workers; they shifted the character of the Church from a small and mainly rural Church, to a large and mainly urban Church. The Irish clergy followed the migrants and continue to do so; the Catholic Church in England is still heavily dependent upon Ireland to supply the priests needed to serve the people. Should the Irish become unable or unwilling to produce the usual supply of 'mission' priests, the Catholic Church in England would be faced with a major manpower crisis, and its ultimate situation might become like that of South America where the indigenous population has never been able to supply its own priests. No doubt such a crisis could be met by a very different deployment of clerical personnel, but it would require a major upheaval of existing structures.

Ever since the Irish famines the Catholic community has been absorbed with the problem of providing Churches and schools for an expanding Catholic population—an expansion which has meant a spiralling pattern of building/debt/collection/building/debt, in which the assets never come anywhere near meeting the capital needs. In this situation the Church is 'poor' almost by definition; a definition which can be indefinitely maintained by manipulation, since the level of experienced poverty is directly related to the way in which the community needs are themselves defined. The decision not merely to retain Catholic schools, but to work towards a situation in which all Catholic children (instead of the present two-thirds) have places in Catholic schools, is by itself quite sufficient to ensure 'poverty' for any foreseeable future. This is because, quite apart from any other consideration, national educational policies (such as the raising of the statutory school leaving age) are likely to keep the actual capital cost per school place in a state of constant expansion; so that it becomes necessary to run very fast indeed merely to stay in the same place. In much the same way there are somehow never quite enough churches, or they are not in the right places, or they are not quite grand enough.

It is clear that the momentum of the Catholic building programme derives from a past situation very different from that which prevails today. The desire to create a set of physical structures which would serve to preserve and foster the faith of the people, as well as to cater in some measure for their material welfare, had a reality value in 1850 that it lacks today. Continued migration, which is typically into the most deprived section of the community, still gives the programme sufficient face validity to make any serious questioning of the assumptions upon which it is based exceedingly difficult.

The channelling of effort and involvement into this overall programme of building, with its attendant debts, serves to keep alive the image of a Church which is poor and struggling; while at the same time it provides a set of concrete goals and tangible achievements. But it has other consequences: it necessarily isolates Catholics from the other Christian communions which have chosen other options and other goals, and it generates a general attitude towards social and political questions which is biased by self-interest. Catholics may therefore appear to be much less concerned with, for example, the quality of educational programmes and legislation than with protecting and fostering their own 'rights'.

This is a typical minority group situation and outlook. Given the stresses of poverty, social disadvantage and well-nigh universal prejudice, loyalty to the group becomes the primary virtue. Those who attempt to 'pass' into WASP (White Anglo-Saxon Protestants) society are seen as disloyal, they are commonly berated for allowing 'human respect' (or gross self-interest) to determine their actions and they are seen as lacking the courage to defend the faith and take the consequencs. Open apostasy is the final and unforgiveable sin: charitable people will try to excuse it, often in terms of unbearable social or psychological strain, but this is only a kindly gloss on the more general assumption that the apostate (like those who took the oath of Supremacy in the sixteenth century)[5] is buying for himself a life of worldly ease and advantage at the price of his immortal soul.

This way of responding is typical of a minority group under pressure: the open question is how long can this kind of evaluation continue to make any real sense? In the 1970s the objective reality is that, in general terms, apostasy will do very few people indeed the slightest good, socially, financially or professionally; it is also true that as a whole Catholics no longer suffer anything more than a marginal degree of material or social disadvantage.[6] With every decade that passes there is more and more evidence that Catholics have become socially mobile, that a substantial Catholic middle-class has emerged, that Catholics are now found in professions that were once closed to them and that few people are discriminated against by virtue of their religion alone. Residual prejudice no doubt exists, but even where it is openly avowed there are very few contexts in which it could be admitted as a 'reasonable' ground for discrimination against an individual.[7]

If one remembers that one of the most important forces maintaining a minority group is the reality of the oppression it experiences at the hands of the majority, it would seem that objectively speaking membership of the Catholic Church should be considered to be elective rather than mandatory. There are plenty of signs that this change has in fact had extensive consequences and repercussions within the church, particularly among educated Catholics who, because of their experience in universities, business and the professions, are most keenly aware of the fact that they are not being discriminated against.[8] The naïve person would assume that this changed situation would be easily recognized and a matter for some rejoicing. Such a person would however fail to see what a profound threat this liberalization offers to the identity and existence of the minority group. The values and mores of the minority were not formed overnight. Families that have retained the faith through hundreds of years of persecution (and this applies quite as much to the Irish as to the English element), converts who have sacrificed their jobs and their social position for the 'true faith', are not psychologically attuned to polite indifference, rather they are geared to fighting for survival and motivated by myths of past and future grandeur: they need an enemy to provide their internal equilibrium as a thirsty horse needs water. It could even be said that they need to suffer, as the ultimate self-justification.[9] This is a dangerous frame of mind since it can result in a more or less paranoid search for an enemy, any enemy, who can be used to justify not merely existing attitudes and beliefs, but also actions which would otherwise be self-evidently aggressive, selfish or dishonest. To some extent a successful symbiosis has existed in England between the Humanists and the Catholics, both have been prepared to think of one another as the embodiment of evil and continuous skirmishing over public policy (religious education, divorce, abortion, etc.) gives to both bodies a *raison d'être* in terms of an 'enemy' to overcome. It is worth noting that for many members of both groups such engagements seem increasingly unreal and they become more and more unwilling to take them seriously.

A group under threat will be willing to accept an authoritarian pattern of leadership and to put up with all the psychological discomforts which the 'emergency' seems to justify. Once the threat is removed people become more critical of despotic patterns of leadership, more unwilling to sacrifice themselves unnecessarily and more willing to question the goals and aspirations of their group, they will resist arbitrary decisions and divide into rival factions.[10] The Reformation created an 'emergency' situation in the Catholic Church, and, with the Counter-Reformation, the Church entered a centuries-long period of embattlement characterized by extreme rigidity, an exaggerated emphasis on conformity, a vertical communications system and an extreme centralization of power in Rome. Although, with the passing of the centuries, the real temporal and political power of the Church declined steadily the aspirations do not appear to have declined at the same rate, the trappings of power remain: the Secretariat of State, ambassadors, Concordats and even a token army. Preparatory work for the second Vatican Council appears to have been carried forward in the full spirit of the Counter-Reformation disturbed by nothing more than a few rumours that the natives were restless and must be quieted by some renewed show of power and, perhaps, a few concessions.

The actual progress of the Council made it clear that, whatever the feeling in Rome, for the rest of the Church the emergency created by the Reformation was decisively over and the measures taken to counter that emergency no longer tolerable. English Catholics were, taking it by and large, as surprised by the progress of the Council as any staff of a Sacred Congregation in Rome; absorbed in their own concerns and dreaming fitfully of the conversion of England, they were almost universally ignorant of the radical content of continental theology and of the growing discontent with the *status quo* abroad.

The second Vatican Council did in fact, in spite of the best efforts of the ecclesiastical bureaucrats, and to the astonishment of the English church, open the door to a programme of self-assessment and re-examination which by itself invited the suggestion that the enemy within the gates was more important now than the enemy without. Pope John XXIII was apparently singularly free of the siege mentality and the authoritarian despotism that this invites; he was not, as has frequently been noted, particularly radical in his theological position—indeed if anything he was rather conservative theologically—but he was unusually open emotionally and intellectually. Since the essence of democratic leadership lies not merely in a willingness to communicate freely with subordinates but also in the further willingness to allow them to communicate freely with one another, it can be seen that Pope John XXIII interpreted the papal office in a democratic way. In a democratic pattern of leadership the responsibility for planning and decision-making is shared and this necessarily means allowing the subordinates to argue, to put opposing points of view, to explore weaknesses as well as merits. To put such a programme into action, however traditional the mechanism used, is to invite a panic reaction in those who have been conditioned to an extreme form of authoritarianism. It is also to invite a measure of seeming chaos, since autocracy is always more tidy than democracy.

Just as it was the better educated section of the Catholic Church in England that had been the first to recognize that active prejudice had largely given way to indifference, so also it was the better educated section which first became aware, albeit belatedly, of the changing theological climate on the Continent, which followed the Vatican Council with the greatest interest[11] and which most easily understood the implications of the Council as evidence of a changing view of authority in the Church; and this was true whether they were in sympathy with the changes or opposed to them.

Following the Council a bitter clash of ideologies emerged within the previously tightly united Catholic Church in England, a clash made all the more bitter because it was so unexpected. On the one hand a group of people emerged who deplored all change, who regarded resistance to such change as an essential virtue; for them the Church is still a beleaguered minority which gets its orders from Rome (itself beleaguered, with the Pope a prisoner) and promulgates them through a militaristic chain of command; any sign that Rome itself is changing is taken to be a sign of weakness, of decay, attributable to the work of the Devil. On the other hand are those who see the Church as an essentially elective group in which everyone has some right to be heard and some duty to follow his conscience even when this may mean opposing 'legitimate' authority. For this group the traditional virtue of loyalty is no adequate response to the needs of the modern world and they have become disenchanted with the task of providing Catholic copies of every worthwhile undertaking from marriage guidance to famine relief; they want evidence that the changes in the Church are truly radical and not mere tinkering with the system.

The Catholic bishops are caught somewhere between these ideologies and give every sign of discomfort; for the most part they have bowed to necessity and have attempted to implement the democratization of the Church in the traditional authoritarian manner. The bishops are officially opposed to liturgical experiment but continuously introduce changes in the liturgy (no doubt suggested by experiments elsewhere) regardless of whether they are locally welcome; such changes are sometimes dramatic but often trivial— they are however invariably attributed to outside intervention, whether it be 'ordered by Rome' or agreed by some remote conference of 'authorities'. As required, they set up parochial, diocesan or national councils with lay bodies to represent everybody, but since the object of the exercise is to set them up, rather than to use them, these are often 'Micky Mouse' organizations which lack any real power or decision-making functions—they usually 'advise'. The Bishops beseech the laity to be loyal and they more or less openly browbeat the clergy by offering those who display signs of discontent the choice between getting out and shutting up.[12]

The Catholic Bishops have under the same overall programme of complicance with 'official policy' become overtly ecumenical in outlook, engaging in modest expressions of mutual goodwill with other Christian bodies and permitting the 'faithful' to engage in inter-denominational carol services, allowing occasional exchanges of pulpits or adequately chaperoned visits to places of worship belonging to other communions. At the same time the cause of the Forty Martyrs has been so vigorously pursued as to have achieved their canonization, thus urging upon the faithful an example of 'loyalty' which, however admirable, is also as obsolete as the hansom cab!

What the body of the faithful makes of all this no one knows and no one seems concerned to find out; all activists both official and unofficial are sure everyone else (except the 'tiny minority' of their opponents) thinks and feels as they do and they are at least united in a general determination to make wild guesses rather than attempt to find out the, possibly embarrassing, truth.

There are, however, other factors at work which may in the end turn out to be much more important than the internal struggles outlined in the preceding paragraphs. More than most other Christian communions in England, Catholics have been isolated from the massive drift towards secularization which has emptied the churches over the last fifty years. Sociological forces which served to encapsulate Catholics as a minority group depended upon a more or less general conviction that religion mattered, that religious belief had social and political consequences which affected the well-being of the body politic—a conviction which evidently very generally prevails in Ulster today. It is the loss, in England, of that general conviction, not a change in its content, which has lifted the long siege. Deprived of the bracing stimuli of ridicule, hatred and contempt, Catholics too may drift down the long road from burning conviction to complete indifference.

It is of course argued that the separate school system provides just that measure of voluntary apartheid which will preserve the Catholic faithful from the well-nigh universal indifference, as it once more or less preserved them from religious intolerance. There is evidence however that Catholic schools will not by themselves preserve or even foster religious conviction, it is already widely recognized that they will do so only when the child's family provides a background in which religious belief is important and religious commitment something more than notional. From this it would seem to follow that if adult Catholics become indifferent, their children will be equally or more indifferent; Catholic school or no Catholic school.

The real question that remains is how Catholics will face the forces of secularization in the next generation; whether they will choose to join Harvey Cox in the secular city, whether they will belatedly show the pattern of vaguely Christian agnosticism which is fashionable today, whether they will embrace some form of religious revival, or whether they will merely wither gently away, remains to be seen. It does seem highly improbable that they can continue to see their membership of the Church as an inescapable legacy of their heredity; it must become more and more obvious that this is a matter for personal decision and that if indeed they dissent, they do so by choice.

Answers to questions about the future of the Catholic Church in England depend not merely on the church itself, but increasingly on broader social forces, in particular the extent to which secularization proceeds within the total culture. Even if it turns out that secularization is a self-limiting process, giving place at some point to a renewed religious sense, the future remains obscure because this is no guarantee in itself for the survival of any particular set of religious structures or for modes of worship which derive their form from tradition. A renewal of the social pressures which make for disadvantage and disability would probably even now revive the all but dead fires of Catholic mediaeval romanticism, but on the present evidence such a turn of events is highly improbable.

The situation of the Catholic Church in England might then be summed up by saying that the Church is in transition from a disadvantaged minority group, whose membership was determined largely by a combination of descent and dissent, to an elective group whose membership is determined by free choice in a relatively open situation. This change must in some measure involve a change from an intense sense of group loyalty, as the ultimate virtue, together with a high tolerance for a rigidly authoritarian pattern of leadership, to a greater concern for the meaning and relevance of religious belief and worship, and the emergence of a more democratic style of leadership. Given the secularization of contemporary society it is not easy to predict to what extent such a change will prove to be the mere decay of an institution which has served its purpose, or on the other hand the long delayed beginning of that second spring for which John Henry Newman hoped so ardently.

NOTES

[1] Because it is cumbersome to use the term Roman Catholic throughout the paper it has been shortened to Catholic in places, but the term is

always used to designate Church membership and never to differentiate a theological position.

2 John L. Thomas, *Religion and the American People* (The Newman Press Maryland 1963).

3 The now classical study by Adorno *et al.* entitled *The Authoritarian Personality* (Harper, New York 1950) or Gordon Allport's major work on *The Nature of Prejudice* (Beacon Press, Boston 1954) have more or less defined the field; there are follow up studies by English psychologists which, however excellent in themselves, are of only secondary importance.

4 The term 'recusant' is usually used to describe those persons or groups of persons who refused to comply with the law, to take the oath of supremacy and/or attend Anglican services and who maintained adherence to the Catholic faith and took part in Catholic worship throughout the time when this was illegal.

5 It is part of the unquestioned group mythology that no one would have taken this oath from conviction, but that all of those who did so did it to save their skins. This may sound very sweeping but it is, once again, fairly typical of the view of the majority group that a minority group will entertain as a reassurance of the moral superiority of their own group.

6 The combination of the 1944 Education Act and the post-war practice of giving maintenance grants to students who obtained university places has been the main means of changing the picture. It is true that some disadvantage undoubtedly remains, but the reason for this seems to be the academic mediocrity of some Catholic schools and the lack of conviction that academic values really matter, together with the more obvious effects of continued migration. In the case of migrants the disadvantage is usually multiply determined and religion is not an important factor.

7 Obviously this discussion applies only to England and specifically excludes the situation in Ulster.

8 Not everyone is ready to abandon the idea that they are being discriminated against, it is too powerful an alibi for personal failure to be given up by everyone; successful people obviously find it easier to see the truth.

9 According to Festinger's theory of Cognitive Dissonance people value very highly anything they have suffered or struggled to retain or attain. The experience of pain gives them a measure of the value of that for which they have endured the pain; the idea that one has suffered needlessly in a worthless cause is extremely threatening to a person's self-esteem. This does not make it any less true that people are usually prepared to suffer for what they believe to be true or worthwhile, but it does explain why persecution effectively reinforces just those beliefs it is designed to erradicate. Cf. L. Festinger, *A Theory of Cognitive Dissonance* (Row Peterson, Evanston 1957).

10 Dictators and authoritarian rulers recognize this well enough and frequently contrive 'Emergency' situations in order to make themselves and their regimen more acceptable.

[11] The excellent coverage of the Council offered by both *The Times* and *Guardian* made it relatively easy for readers of these papers to get a very good idea not merely of the events of the Council but also of the internal political groupings and their manoevres. At the same time the popular press and the mass media generally, while they did not cover the Council so closely, did give a great deal of very sympathetic coverage to Pope John and in this way probably did an enormous amount to change the public image of Catholicism in England.

[12] The most striking example of this in recent years was the way in which the Papal Encyclical letter *Humanae Vitae* was used as a test case for clerical loyalty. In the diocese of Nottingham mere silence was not enough; clergy who failed to give interior assessment to this document were arbitrarily and apparently permanently removed from circulation by a variety of devices. Other dioceses, proceeding with greater caution but steady pressure for conformity in this matter, removed a number of well known priests from the official ranks of the clergy over the next couple of years —most of them left 'voluntarily' and quietly. Of course a policy such as this does pay some dividends, since it removes vocal and independent priests from the scene, things become rather quieter, but it is doubtful whether they become any 'better'.

Methodism and Society

JOHN LAMPARD

THE RELATIONSHIP between Methodism and society has been a complex and controversial one in the two and a half centuries since its beginning. This chapter can only offer a generalized outline of the subtle interplay, concentrating on the social origins of Methodism, the causes of ninteenth-century divisions and the reasons for twentieth-century unification.

The creation of Methodism, according to that Church's mythology, began with the conversion of John Wesley, a devout High Anglican priest and failed missionary. The Anglican Church, the myth says, was in a state of total disarray and apostasy, apart from a few devout High Anglicans who remained true to the faith. It is of course in the interests of both the Anglo-Catholics and the Methodists to denigrate the established church of the time to legitimate their divisions and to enable them to show that they were the saviours of eighteenth-century Christianity. More recent historical research has tended to deny this part of the myth and has painted a kinder picture of the state of the Church at that time.

At a fellowship service at Aldersgate Street, in 1738, Wesley experienced his conversion. In his own words, 'About a quarter before nine, while he (the preacher) was describing the change which God works in the heart through faith in Christ, I felt my heart strangely warmed. I felt I did trust in Christ, Christ alone for salvation.'

The myth continues that from this point onwards nothing could hold Wesley back, in the salvation of England. Preaching in the open air, to the roughest and poorest of the land, from Kingswood miners to Yorkshire woolspinners, thousands were soundly converted and the Methodist Church grew. Wesley did not want to secede from the Anglican Church, but his success and his followers made it inevitable. Wesley transformed a totally irreligious country to one filled with the praise of God. The clear parallels between this version of the beginning of Methodism and the opening chapters of the Book of Acts cannot be missed.

The influence of this myth has pervaded many works of Church history because until recently Church historians have generally failed to answer, or indeed ask, questions about the prevailing social conditions and their influence on nascent Methodism. Church history has been written along biographical lines, with too much emphasis on personalities (although the complex personality of John Wesley himself has in the main been considered too sacred for scrutiny). Church historians have not examined sufficiently the sociological and economic situation which existed in Wesley's day, attributing too much of his success to his spiritual genius, his theology and his organizational ability, important as these may be.

The first person to attempt to relate the origins of Methodism to societal movements was the French historian Elie Halévy, whose uncommitted background enabled him to see new perspectives.[1] He attacked the myth of an irreligious society and suggested the protestant dissenting feeling still ran deep in society. He is supported in this view by another historian, E. P. Thompson, who says,

> The intellectual history of Dissent is made up of collisions, schisms, mutations; and one feels often that the dormant seeds of political Radicalism lie within it, ready to germinate whenever planted in a beneficial and hopeful social context.[2]

The social context of the late 1730s was one of national violence and upheaval in the chaotic and anarchic days of early industrialization. It is not easy for modern Methodists to appreciate the tense social atmosphere which was the breeding ground of Methodism. Halévy says that an economic crisis towards the end of the 1730s, caused partly by overproduction, could have plunged the country into violent revolution, but instead it was the key to the modern erruption of evangelicalism.

There is evidence, Halévy says, that it was in the areas of the most acute economic crisis, where there were riots, insurrections and social chaos, such as the area south of Bristol and the industrial villages of Yorkshire, that there was most evidence of religious crisis and growth. As he says, 'the despair of the working classes was the raw material to which Methodist doctrine and discipline gave a shape'.

Halévy developed his thesis in later works, to argue that England was spared a violent counterpart to the French Revolution, first by the initial Revival started by Wesley and George Whitfield in 1739 and later during the tumultuous years 1789–1815 by the success of Methodism.[3]

The problem with a sweeping thesis like Halévy's lies in either proving or disproving it. Exactly the same problem arises with Weber's and Tawney's thesis that protestantism was the driving force behind the growth of capitalism. In their attempts to examine the growth of Methodism in relation to the society in which it flowered, several different positions have been taken by historians. These positions can be plotted on a cross-shaped grid. The horizontal axis measures degrees of influence (Methodism had pivotal influence on society, to little or no influence) while the vertical axis shows their judgement as to whether the growth of Methodism was beneficial and elevating to society or damaging, and crushing.

Halévy, along with the majority of Methodist historians, argues that the influence was great and that it was beneficial. It brought stability and meaning to society at a crucial and difficult time. Halévy asks the question why, after the initial violence of the working classes at the beginning of the nineteenth century, this petered out and became mystical and conservative. The answer he believes lies in the fact that when there is a revolutionary situation the proletariat look for ideals to the bourgeoisie (middle-class citizens). At the time of potential revolution in England, the bourgeoisie were not feeling revolutionary as they had been filled with the doctrines of an anti-revolutionary and conservative faith. Methodist influence crept by a sort of osmosis into all ranks of society and gave rise to the many voluntary associations which sprang up. If people felt they ought to do something to improve the situation, and their faith and experience tell them that they can, then they will not be revolutionary. Methodism thus benefited society.

The best statement of the alternative maximizing view comes from E. P. Thompson whose hard-hitting polemic attempts to show that the influence of Methodism was repressive, evil, crushing and disastrous for the hopes of the working classes.[4] Thompson, it should be mentioned, received a childhood innoculation against things Methodist by attending a Methodist Church, but beneath his excessive language lies an argument which should at least be listened to.

He says there is support for Halévy's thesis that Methodism prevented revolution, but that the means it used to achieve it were harmful. The two aspects of early Methodism which fascinate him were the two, apparently contradictory, experiences of a deep desire for discipline and good order, and marked religious enthusiasm in worship. Methodism, he argues was the ideal 'tool' for encouraging submission by the new working classes.

> Methodism is most remarkable during the war years for two things; first, its gains were greatest among the new industrial working class: second ... ministers ... regarded it as their duty to manipulate the submissiveness of their followers and to discipline all deviant growths within the Church which could give offence to authority.[5]

Methodism, Thompson says, was uniquely suited, by reason of its emphasis on the values of discipline and of order, to appeal to mill owners, manufacturers and foremen. It provided an internalized discipline for its followers, who did not need so much external discipline. In other words, Methodism served as an ideological means of self-justification for the new masters, and a means of inner regulation for the workers. The role of worship was crucial because it met the need of the new oppressed class for somewhere where they could expel their pent up psychic energy. Instead of channelling it into revolutionary fervour (as no doubt Thompson would like them to have done) they put it into emotional revival and camp meetings.

Thompson has rightly been criticized for presenting a very ideological and unbalanced picture of early nineteenth-century Methodism, but he offers perspectives which cannot be ignored. There is little need to explain why his interpretation has so upset traditional church historians, but they equally do not like the way in which Methodist history has been treated by historians who range themselves at the other end of the scale. John Kent, for example, has argued that the impact of Methodism was small compared to other social forces. He claims that the maximizers 'seem to exaggerate the effect of denominational allegiance on behaviour; they also accept too uncritically the assumption that nineteenth-century Methodism can be treated as a single, compact, organic historical force'.[6] The much flaunted links between Methodism and the trade unions, he says, are much exaggerated.

The minimizing view is supported by many secular historians of the nineteenth century who demote Methodist history to a chapter of its own, unrelated to the 'real' events of social and historical importance. They doubt if it had much influence at all, and are thus little interested if the social effect was beneficial or malevolent.

What is not generally disputed is that Methodism presented two very different faces to the world. On the one hand, as it spread among working class people in a time of possible revolution, it was seen by some as a possible force for sedition, while on the other it was patently never politically revolutionary. Wesley himself was a Tory who recommended, among other things, the subjugation of the American colonialists. If one wants to look for psychological reasons, Wesley may have been reacting to the unfortunate experiences he suffered in America as a young man. It should also not be forgotten that during his childhood his father's rectory was more than once attacked by enraged mobs, and may have been set on fire by an opponent. Such an experience would not unnaturally encourage a person towards the need in society for good order and discipline. Within his own personality Wesley was able to contain the apparent contradictions which his preaching and practice illustrate. Dr B. Semmel has recently come to the defence of Wesley by demonstrating that theologically he was able to hold two different attitudes together. Wesley preached universal salvation and the place of everyone in it, but at the same time said that people must be obedient to duly authorized authority, be it Church or State.[7]

By force of personality and sheer hard work Wesley was able to hold these differing attitudes together within Methodism, but after his death in 1791 it was only a matter of time before the inherent tensions in his theology and churchmanship began to produce divisions within Methodism. The delicate balance maintained by Wesley between autocracy and democracy could not be maintained under the social impact of the French Revolution. Methodism contained within itself those who wanted to see a truly democratic church, which could have nothing to do with the Established Church, and those who still saw union with the Established Church as a hoped-for possibility.

Under pressure from the democratizers, a Plan of Pacification was worked out in 1795 which left final power with the preachers meeting together in Conference, but gave local churches a measure of democratic rights. This was insufficient for the Rev. Alexander Kilham, who led the first important secession in 1797, although not a great number of people left with him to form the New Connexion (as opposed to the Old Connexion which soon became known as Wesleyan Methodism). The New Connexion developed a more democratic structure and included in its numbers the more radical element influenced by the writings of Tom Paine. In fact, in Huddersfield members of the New Connexion were known as 'Tom Paine Methodists'. This radical and possibly pro-revolutionary wing of Methodism never expanded greatly, containing only 8,000 members in 1811.

It must be appreciated that what looks mild and harmless today was seen as being dangerous and subversive around the turn of the century. The tight organizational structure, with local societies, circuits, districts, a Conference and itinerant preachers meant that communication within the institution was fast and efficient. To people fearful of the excesses of the French Revolution, anything which apparently flourished among the potentially revolutionary classes was to be abhorred. In 1800 the Bishop of Rochester stated that sedition and atheism were the real object of Methodism. In 1811 a Bill was brought before Parliament to ban Methodist preachers, both itinerant and local, for fear of revolution. It was not dropped until the Archbishop of Canterbury intervened on behalf of Methodism. To opponents one Methodist looked very like another, be he Old Connexion or New.

Methodism grew at a rapid rate in the counter-revolutionary years after 1795, particularly among the artisan working people. The Conference made every effort to show that it was not a radical or revolutionary movement and to this day it begins its annual activities by sending a message of loyalty to the Queen.

The further divisions within Methodism in the first half of the nineteenth century can be seen in a number of perspectives, as it reacted to the changing society in which it existed. The struggles between central authority and local democratic rights was a direct parallel with the contemporary social movements. The divisions can also be seen as the growing pains of what was, sociologically, still a sect as it attempted to become a church (but stuck halfway as a denomination) or thirdly in terms of a desire for social respectability and acceptance versus a radical spirit attempting to remain true to its imagined roots.

The second, and most serious division within Methodism, can perhaps best be seen in terms of this third perspective. The Rev. Hugh Bourne, reverting to the outdoor style of preaching adopted by Wesley, came under displeasure for the emotionalism of his religious gatherings. Copying the American 'Camp Meetings' he attracted large numbers of people, who camped out in some remote place, for several days, interspersing revival addresses with prayer meetings. Large numbers of people, in out of the way places, smacked of sedition and Wesleyan Methodism saw this as a threat to its desire for respectability. After being expelled from the Wesleyans, Bourne formed the Society of Primitive Methodists, together with a like-mind spirit, the Rev. William Clowes in 1812. By the mid-1850s Primitive Methodists numbered over 100,000.

The third major division came in 1815 when William O'Bryan finally broke away from the Wesleyan Methodists (after having once been expelled and readmitted) to form the Bible Christians which developed in rural areas west of Bristol. Again, this division can be seen in terms of the tension within Methodism between authority and democracy. It was in the Methodist breakaway groups that the struggle towards democracy made itself felt, and among them women were first authorized as itinerant. (It was over forty years after the different branches of Methodism united in 1932 that women were ordained into the ministry.) The very titles taken by the seceding Methodists, 'Primitive' and 'Bible Christians' indicate a desire for a sort of unity with the past, when the tradition was pure and unsullied.

There was a tendency for Wesleyan Methodism to be untroubled by the comparative successes of the religious groups which had seceded, because as the years went by the Wesleyans grew in number, totalling 200,000 in 1820.

Maldwyn Edwards has classified the social and political attitude of Methodism in the first half of the nineteenth century as one of dominant Toryism and underlying liberalism.[8] There is ample evidence for the dominance of a conservative attitude from the Methodist hierarchy. Their response to the crucial Reform movements between 1817 and 1832 was summarized by a statement made at a Conference a few years earlier, when the members were told, 'Fear the Lord and the King and meddle not with them that are given to change'. When the Tolpuddle Martyrs were arrested an appeal was made to the Secretary of Conference, the Rev. Jabez Bunting, for help. He was either too busy or too reluctant to grant an interview and no influence was offered to help the men. This lack of sympathy with working-class aspirations was a necessary part of Methodism's desire to become a respected and accepted part of society, but it cost it dear in society's attitude towards it. Methodism fell between two stools, it was rejected by the ruling class who mocked it, while pleased to receive its constant professions of loyalty, and was rejected by the working class who saw it as an ally and supporter of an illiberal and unjust social system.

It would be wrong, however, to judge Methodism in this formative time solely on the strength or weakness of its Toryism. The underlying liberalism, which came to the fore towards the end of the century, had strong social roots, although it is possible to claim that it was also a product of Methodist theology. Edwards argues convincingly that the Toryism of the first part of the eighteenth century had to give way to liberalism because Methodism and liberalism both drew their strength from the same areas, where the new industrial middle-class lived. Methodism drew away from the Toryism of the Established Church (and was repulsed by the Anglo-Catholic movement) and allied itself more with the old Dissenting groups, regarding itself as Nonconformist.

In the second half of the nineteenth century the dramatic periods of growth in membership, which were characteristic of the earlier years of Methodism, gave way to a period of steady slow growth and then decline after the end of the century. It is impossible to offer monocausal explanations for the vicissitudes in Methodist membership. The periods of marked public excitement, such as 1832–3, when the Wesleyans increased their membership by 9.3 per cent, were not so marked in the second half of the century, and economic factors may have had some effect.

Methodist leaders had no doubts as to what caused deficiencies in the growth rate. Currie quotes the incoming President of 1895 as saying, 'Nothing has more effectively hindered the progress of Christianity than the absence of that oneness for which the Saviour prayed',[9] a judgement which, perhaps, displays a lack of understanding of world Church history.

It was in Methodism that the English ecumenical movement has its roots, and some Methodists have seen in the ecumenical movement a new criteria for 'success' now that membership statistics no longer show increases. Just as denominationalism has social origins, so too has ecumenism. Wilson argues that 'organisations amalgamate when they are weak, rather than when they are strong, since alliance means compromise and amendment of commitment'.[10] Ecumenism is thus the religious response to a sense of weakness in society. His arguments disturb those who only want to see theological motives for ecumenism.

In the first part of the twentieth century the different parts of Methodism, particularly at a ministerial level, could see little to keep themselves apart. Currie argues, rightly, that the processes of division within Methodism generally brought into being movements which conferred more authority on laymen, while the processes of amalgamation reduced lay authority and increased centralized and ministerial authority. In 1907 the United Methodist Free Church (itself the result of an earlier union), the Bible Christians and the New Connexion came together to form the United Methodist Church. A quarter of a century later they joined with the Primitives and the Wesleyans to form the present Methodist Church. Economic forces played their part, for the post-war years had taken their toll on the resources of the weaker United Methodists and the Primitives. They voted decisively for union, while the stronger Wesleyan just managed the necessary majority.

The vast social changes of the twentieth century have produced no new religious movement of the significance of Methodism in the last two centuries. Ecumenism has been the only religious response and in the last few years attempts to unite Methodism with the Church of England have failed. Perhaps people have seen the basic bankruptcy of ecumenism. The high hopes of Methodist Union were short lived and combined membership which stood at about one million at the turn of the century is now almost half that figure.

* *

The multitude of social forces which helped give rise to Methodism, to divide it, and to unite it, continue to influence everyone's life, but it is not at all clear how they will interact with Methodism, in the future.

NOTES

[1] Elie Halévy, *The Birth of Methodism in England*, Trans. and Ed. B. Semmel (University of Chicago Press 1971).

[2] E. P. Thompson, *The Making of the English Working Class*, p. 39 (Penguin 1968).

[3] Elie Halévy, *History of the English People in 1815* (Penguin).

[4] E. P. Thompson, op. cit.

[5] Ibid., p. 386.

[6] John Kent, in *The Pelican Guide to Modern Theology Vol. 2*, p. 306 (Penguin 1969).

[7] Bernard Semmel, *The Methodist Revolution* (Heinemann 1974).

[8] Maldwyn Edwards, *After Wesley* (Epworth Press 1935).

[9] Robert Currie, *Methodism Divided*, p. 97 (Faber and Faber 1968).

[10] Bryan Wilson, *Religion in Secular Society*, p. 152 (Penguin 1969).

2—DAD * *

2

THE CHURCH

Trevor Rowe and John Todd

The Church

JOHN M. TODD

ONE COULD ask whether there is any consistent definition given to the word 'church' among Christians of any one of the larger communions. One might ask whether a common factor can be found to identify a church in England today as the same thing as the church in, say, fifteenth-century England, or third-century North Africa. One can adduce at least one factor without any further ado that spans all places and times. Christians have one constant pole within their frame of reference. The New Testament presents a text which is unchanging; like other texts, written by particular people at a particular time. The variety of available manuscripts prompts revisions now and then. But the verbal symbols are not for the most part in dispute. They are there. The texts concern events which are alleged to have occurred not very long before the texts were written down. Whatever their precise literary and historical status Christians believe that the experience of the Christians who composed them was something unique, that the events referred to were also unique and that these writings provide a religious norm.

At the heart of this writing lies the consciousness of the writers that they are members of a special community. This consciousness has continued among Christians till the present time. There has been a historical continuity of Christians and a continuity of communities which they created and which created them. These communities have commonly been called churches, and later the Church. In trying to understand this community of theirs Christians have invariably returned to the New Testament, and to some extent to the Old Testament, using these texts in a great variety of ways as normative. The attempt to penetrate these writings more fully and to understand their message for the Church and for all men has never ceased. Thus whatever the effect of other factors there will also be a tendency among Christians of the most varying individual traditions to converge in their understanding of the Church. For they all return to these normative biblical texts.

From the beginning Christians were faced with a new problem. They had the Judaic sense of their community as holistic, a community elect of God, chosen out. But they no longer had the Old Testament and in particular the Law, the Torah, to guide them in all matters of daily behaviour from worship to morals. Inevitably a new structure grew up enabling them to identify themselves and to control the community, and to express their faith in Christ and his saving action. If all they needed to do was to meet and break bread together, still they had to decide how, where, and when to do it. So the Spirit was submitted to rules.

We often read back into the middle ages a Roman Catholic theory of a highly structured Church. But the reality was not exactly as it is often imagined. If it was, Aquinas must have written a treatise *De Ecclesia* which he did not. Canon Law, controlled from Rome, structured all aspects of religious behaviour, in a kind of Old Testament model. But there was still no thorough theory of the Church, or a theology of the Church to support it. The Church was not thought out as the coherent thing it later was. It was rather an evolving complex of aspects of the lives of Europeans, of that single Christendom within which everyone recognized that the Pope and the bishops had responsibility for the spiritual aspects of life and all that pertained to them. With the gradual increase in efficiency at all levels it became possible for this control to be more and more strict and to reach further both geographically and socially and psychologically. And as it did so, proliferating in more and more rules, underwritten by Rome's quasi-divine authority, so movements critical of this activity became increasingly insistent, basing themselves on the New Testament in depth, and in general wishing to oppose the papal interpretation of texts such as that 'I am Peter' which Rome was using to 'prove' its authority from Scripture.

Increasing numbers of people were impressed by the case which many 'heretics' had put forward that the gospel was betrayed when the 'spiritual' was controlled in this fashion. So polarization increased between the established structured Church and 'spirituals' of a wide variety. It led inevitably to the Reformation, a Europewide revolution in favour of 'gospel' and against 'law'; *the gospel* of the New Testament text being increasingly available in the vernacular, in print in the second half of the fifteenth century—*the law* of the papal bureaucracy, ever developing its scope and claims.

Following on that cataclysmic polarization the two poles have been drawing nearer to each other throughout the following 400 years. A theology of the Church has been slowly emerging, which takes us back to Paul and to Augustine. Catholics have experienced a slowly increasingly conviction that the spiritual and biblical element must lie at the heart of any ecclesial reality. On the other hand the reformed traditions have experienced a slowly increasing conviction of the importance of structure. In any society of human beings, however much that society may have a spiritual or religious purpose, organization is unavoidable. It is sometimes said that Methodist ministers are some of the most closely controlled of all Christian ministers or presbyters, their deployment being rigorously disciplined by the Annual Conference. Catholics on the other hand are bathing in the climax of an unstructured, evangelical-type movement long in the making. But of course it may well be said that it is precisely against the background of a rigid wide-world structure and ritual practice that it is possible for Catholics to engage in a display of extraordinary freedom and experimentation at every level from public worship to moral conventions. However, an event, totally unexpected, has occurred in the worldwide eruption of the Pentecostalist movement within the bounds of the official Roman Catholic world, a movement often left remarkably uncontrolled by the bishops. It has transformed the style of liturgy throughout large areas; notably in America the eucharist as celebrated in many spheres has been greatly influenced by the relaxed yet fervent style of the Pentecostalist movement, a style which deliberately allows emotions to be expressed, but which is also meditative and biblical. Catholic worship has suffered a permanent change, essentially much greater than that of Vatican II, although it was undoubtedly the style, the discursive sympathetic and biblical style of the Vatican II texts which provided the enabling context.

It is perhaps a cliché association, but I think it is valid to see an analogy between this 'revival' within the Roman Catholic Church and the revival within the Church of England led by John Wesley. All over England and other parts of the British Isles his 'Methodist' groups grew up in villages and towns. My opposite number, Trevor

Rowe, refers to the way in which these groups were to 'control' the religious experience of converts. But whilst any group will in some sense act as a 'control' I think the aspect of mission was as much in evidence as the aspect of discipline. However there is no doubt that traditions of behaviour emerged and the classes must have played a large part in making this possible. It seems to me that in spite of various kinds of decline there still is within Methodism a very strong sense of the local community and some determination to stick to certain fundamental standards of behaviour. In both these senses of the local community and of the importance of public witness the Methodist tradition has much in common with Catholicism even though the content of the respective witnesses may sometimes be in direct contradiction, the Methodists refusing the gambling, and the freedom with alcohol which has tended to characterize Catholic parishes in the past.

But if the Christian witness is to be realized in a single local church, a particular and local realization of the body of Christ, it will need some theology of itself. At this point we may turn to a text of Vatican II, for this and many other similar texts do provide something at least on the way to an understanding of the Church that all the endemic traditions of Christian England could find fruitful. It points back to Augustine and therefore forward to the Kingdom of God at the end of time. The last paragraph of the opening section of the text ('The Mystery of the Church') on 'the Church', from Augustine, sums it up:

'The Church "like a pilgrim, presses forward amid the presecutions of the world and the consolations of God", announcing the cross and death of the Lord until he comes. By the power of the risen Lord it is given strength that it might, in patience and in love, overcome its sorrows and its challenges, both within itself and from without, and that it might reveal to the world, even though dimly, yet faithfully, the mystery of its Lord until, finally, it will be manifested in full light.'

Here we have a doctrine of the Church which combines both a high doctrine of the Church as holy, the symbol of the heavenly Jerusalem, and the doctrines of the secular Church, the straggling men and women, good and bad, the anonymous presence involved in all the insoluble issues of humanity; a Church which brings the sign of its holiness into the market place, which carries its realistic fight for justice and truth even into the place of charity, to the eucharistic worship. It is above all a realistic doctrine: 'The Church is no more "sacred" than the world is "profane": they are both secular'.[1] The Church is operating in time, that time 'between'— between the Christ-events, and the last Day.

Returning to Augustine, but with an eye on a great range of writing about the Church in the last hundred years from Christians of many denominations, and in the present context thinking particularly of two books by Roman Catholics, Kung's *The Church*, but also Louis Bouyer's *L'Eglise de Dieu*, we may well be able to work towards an ecclesiology, based on understandings of the New Testament which is acceptable certainly to Methodists and Catholics, perhaps very much more widely.

Markus, in a passage directly prior to that already quoted, writes of this theology: 'The Church was holy not because it was here and now the congregation of the holy, the unspotted or elect, but because as a community it had an essential relationship with the heavenly city.' But 'here and now the *ecclesia* though holy, must always be a mixed body. In it, as in the "world", the two cities are inextricably intertwined. From this point of view, there is no difference between "Church" and "world". Augustine, deliberately upheld against the Donatists the appropriateness of speaking of the Church in "worldly" terms, and indeed defined the Church as "the world reconciled".

'Augustine saw the Church on earth as having no privileges beyond other secular communities in human society. Both Church and secular community "share the same ultimate ambivalence, the same relativity, the same liability to infection with sin and distortion through betrayal: also, the same possibilities of creative holiness and redeeming love".'

The distinctive Catholic contribution will be to remind us of the high doctrine of the Church as the sign of the heavenly Jerusalem, the holy company of saints in heaven. 'It anticipates the Kingdom as its herald. Although it cannot be identified with the eschatological Kingdom, yet it may be called "the Kingdom of God" or "of Christ" just as the old Jerusalem could be called the "holy City" on account of its symbolic reference.'

So the Church as Catholics see it, both in the most recent restatements at Vatican II, and in the oldest and most central descriptions of the first centuries, is a sign and a symbol. This significant community proclaims the Gospel, preaching the message of the Kingdom established by the crucified Lord. This is done at the liturgical celebration, in sacramental worship, when the Christian community becomes an anticipatory sign of the fully human community of love, which we await in hope. Finally this community services the world, trying to express that redeeming love which brought it into being and which it proclaims.

Thus the Church does not transform societies into the Kingdom of God. It subjects all worldly institutions and programmes to critical scrutiny, and may itself inspire creative initiatives. But always it is the perspective of hope for the coming Kingdom which enables this. Finally we may quote from Augustine words with which Markus ends his book, and which complement those already quoted, taken from the Vatican II text: 'The pilgrim, if he walks in faith, is not yet at home; he is on the way.... Our joy is not yet achieved: it is held in hope.... Yet, let us even now place ourselves in that victory which is still to come....'

NOTE

[1] R. A. Markus, *Saeculum: History and Society in the Theology of St. Augustine* (C.U.P. 1970). The last paragraphs of this chapter are largely inspired by this book.

The Church

TREVOR ROWE

'IF THINE heart is as my heart, if thou lovest God and all
mankind, I ask no more: give me thine hand.' So wrote John
Wesley in his important sermon on *Catholic Spirit*. Although
Wesley makes it clear in that sermon that he is not advocating
theological indifferentism, i.e. it does not matter what you believe,
it is clear that in his order of priorities some things are more important than others. It is very odd that in the discussion of
Anglican/Methodist union some Methodists put such store upon the
compatibility between the proposed scheme and the summary of
Methodist doctrinal standards set out in one section of the *Deed of
Union*. It is odd too that the Methodist Conference in recent years,
on two notable occasions, acted as a doctrinal court and dismissed
two of its ministers for heresy. Odd, because Methodism has always
tended to err in the direction of the general and the diffuse when
it has engaged in defining its doctrinal standards. It has tended to
define its identity as a distinct body in organizational rather than
doctrinal terms.

Wesley was a great eclectic theologian. He had a tremendous
capacity for being able to bring together—sometimes in synthesis,
at other times in creative tension—material from many sources.
This is well described by Gordon Rupp: 'It is through the mind
of John Wesley that the Methodist Revival was coupled with the
historical Church, and it is of importance that into that mind were
woven the richest and most diverse strands of the English Protestant
tradition.'[1] Any modest knowledge of John Wesley indicates how
wide his sympathies were and how diverse his sources of inspiration. He must have been among the most widely read men of his
time. When he came to select material for the *Christian Library*,
intended as a do-it-yourself further education kit for his preachers,
we are shown this. The Fathers, and not least those from the East,
the Reformers, the Puritans, the Caroline divines—the list of his

sources seems almost endless. The Methodist Covenant Service, so highly praised by many non-Methodists, illustrates very well how this eclecticism has worked in a liturgical form.[2]

Methodist roots are catholic in this sense. The actual sources of inspiration were of no account. What mattered was whether a thing was true and cohered with experience. Such an openness of attitude is difficult to maintain—or articulate. In periods of stress it has tended to freeze and defend itself in a neo-orthodoxy—as Lutheranism did. For Methodism it happened in certain periods of the nineteenth century; it was apparent in the threatening situation of possible Anglican/Methodist union; and as it is having to come to terms with the recent, so-called, theological ferment. Methodism has twisted its original catholic spirit into a form of catholic orthodoxy borrowed from the most rigid periods of the Church's history.

The idea of 'dissent and descent' can be linked with theology—with 'dissent' standing for a free, open theologizing and 'descent' for a structuring of acceptable beliefs within defined limits. In order that we can explore the possibility let us assume that Methodism has moved theologically from a position of 'dissent' to 'descent'. Being influenced by both these elements it is interesting to read a book like that of the Catholic theologian Schillebeeckx: *Christ the Sacrament*, in which there is offered a carefully worked out scheme for a doctrine of ministry and sacraments that derives from a doctrine of the Church, which itself derives from a doctrine of Christ. It is this sort of consistency that the 'descent' part of a Methodist wants to embrace. But the 'dissent' part wants to respond with characteristic Methodist pragmatism and see the Church, not in its relation to Christology, but as a response to human need in each generation —underemphasizing continuity in the interests of relevance. Not all Methodists would feel happy with the exuberance, but many would feel an echo within them of the words of a preacher in the Methodist Conference of 1836: 'Methodism piece by piece, as it was wanted, came down from heaven from God.'[3]

There is a wider chasm than most are prepared to recognize and admit between the rank and file Methodist and the ministers of my generation, deeply influenced by men like Newton Flew, Principal for many years of Wesley House, Cambridge. We belonged to the Methodism of the rank and file but, by educational opportunity, we found ourselves with a wider sympathy towards catho-

licism because we had developed wide sympathy for most things—
not knowing how closely we were true sons of Wesley. Flew gave
us a view of catholicity that was both exciting and enriching. How
glad I was personally to turn from the sermons of Wesley to those
of Augustine—from the limited issues of Methodism to the great
issues of the fourth century. All this displayed the imbalance of a
young man at a period of transition, but the vision remains, as I
fancy it does for many of my generation. We look at catholicism
with some of the romance that Newman had. That does not mean
that we like very much the Roman Catholicism we have known.
But we don't dismiss it, in spite of provocations like the encyclical
Humanae Vitae.

There was a rather sickening stage a few years back when
Methodists in order to display their ecumenical virility had to have
a Roman Catholic scalp on their belts. If you reported your
ecumenical exploits you had to include 'and we are getting on very
well with our Roman Catholic friends'. I am sure there was value
in this. But it was a bit phoney. I sensed that Methodists felt safe
with Roman Catholics in ecumenical activity because union with
them seemed remote. Much more dangerous were the Anglicans.
We might unite with them! I hope that the time has now come for
real dialogue that may lead to mutual help in getting out of the
impasse in our development that has suffocated us so much.

There are good reasons why Methodists and Roman Catholics
fit each other congenial, and others we may guess at. I remember
a delightful moment at a conference in Liverpool when Cardinal
Heenan was addressed as 'an eminent nonconformist'. It was a
misuse of words, but it made a point that as ecclesiastical bodies
Methodists and Roman Catholics are minorities and non-
established. A lot of sociological factors lie behind this. The Irish
majority in the Roman Catholic Church is not unlike the working-
class majority of Methodism not too long ago. Certainly it is true
of the young Methodist and Roman Catholic radicals that they
have felt a common bond by both being the products of the
grammar school system and they met at University or afterwards
with a sense of rapport. Working with Anglicans I recognize how
much a family Methodism is in comparison with the Church of
England. Methodism possesses a grape-vine that can communicate

both gossip and care. I understand something similar is true of Roman Catholics.

But are there other things of greater important than these? Much has been made of the Methodist 'class meeting'. The thing that distinguishes Wesley from other revivalist preachers is that he froze the commitment of the new converts by putting them under the conforming pressure of a small group. In other ways he followed the pattern of many others who have secured the radical attitude to change we call conversation. For typically pragmatic reasons— the raising of funds—Wesley developed the class system and found that the primary, face-to-face, groups he had created served to establish the converts in their new way of life. This continued as the great stabilizing force in Methodism for many years. Face-to-face groups continue today in many forms—some more cohesive than others and thus exercising more influence on their members. Only a small proportion of Methodists belong to groups in which they have very close contact with others. Some belong only to the large group of the congregation. The rest may be loosely associated with a guild, women's meeting, etc., which makes no great personal demand on them. What Roman Catholics are discovering is that wherever there are people meeting in small face-to-face groups there is vitality. Though in these groups radical ideas are expressed and stimulated, they do form an association that maintains people within the Church. During a period when, in a number of ways, the imperatives towards Mass attendance have been relaxed, such groups have contributed towards stability of religious practice. For Methodism early and for Roman Catholics lately the small group structure has been seen to be necessary for the vitality of religious life.

At the level of overall church structures the parallels between Methodism and the Roman Catholic Church are more complex. Both have always been centrally directed organizations. In Methodism the centre is the Conference. For Roman Catholics there are two related centres—the Bishop and Rome. Wesley's early autocracy gave way during the nineteenth century to a moderately democratic system whereby the people at the periphery could, by representation, influence the central government of Conference. This still exists and appears to have extended in recent years through the large number of working parties that have been set up to advise on every conceivable subject. This semblance of greater participation is undermined by two factors. One, the population from which membership of these working parties is drawn is quite small—many people serve on a number of them. Two, the subjects concerned are so interrelated that effective action to implement policy can only be achieved by a very few people who have all the strings in their hands. Joy in participation gives way to frustration. Methodists have a book: *The Constitutional Practice and Discipline of the Methodist Church* that includes 987 Standing Orders as well as other documents that govern the life of the Church. Increasingly Methodists are becoming experts at ignoring its requirements. The signs of hope are often to be found happening independently of, or in spite of, the formal structures. I understand that lively things are happening in the Roman Catholic Church independently of the parish and diocesan structures. It is not for me to weigh the various levels of government in the Roman Catholic Church, but my guess would be that in descending order it would go: parish, diocese, Rome, National Church, deanery. In Methodism it would go: circuit, local church, Conference, District. Obviously if Methodists and Roman Catholics are to work together within ecclesiastical structures, the differences in these lists would have to be appreciated. Another point of some importance is that the two Churches are influenced in similar ways by money. Neither has the funds of the Church Commissioners to prop up the system. The availability of money determines most priorities. As the chief part of this derives from local sources in both Churches the opportunity for local policy-making is great, even if it is not taken. Both Churches at the local level could learn the tactical use of money in bringing about desired change.

However much we may build up similarities between the two Churches it cannot be said that on some quite fundamental matters their priorities are the same. In progressive and reactionary Roman Catholicism there is emphasis on worship—even though there may be disagreement about the form it should take. This cannot honestly be said about Methodism. The average Methodist has a very loose attachment to eucharistic worship. In small churches a high proportion of members may communicate once a month. In larger churches the proportion tends to be very small. In spite of the efforts of many enthusiasts it has so far proved impossible to develop in the majority of Methodists even a moderate degree of sacramental devotion. Similarly service to the community lies lower on the agenda for most people than the maintenance of the Christian community. Those who see the future for ecumenicity in developing together a proper emphasis on worship and mission held in appropriate balance must face the fact that Methodism, at least, starts a long way behind.

And yet the resources are all there in her tradition: the high sacramentalism of Wesley, evangelism integrated with service, the small group and so much else. We have retreated on so many grounds that would be attractive to many Roman Catholics today. Perhaps they can help us to recover our past 'dissent'.

NOTES

[1] *The London Quarterly and Holborn Review*, July 1953, p. 167.

[2] David Tripp, *The Renewal of the Covenant in the Methodist Tradition* (London 1969).

[3] E. G. Rupp, op. cit., p. 169.

3

MISSION

Pauline Webb and Cecily Hastings

Mission

CECILY HASTINGS

THERE ARE broad and inspiring statements of the Church's mission which we can derive from scripture: to proclaim the Kingdom of God (while not mistaking itself for it, one of our besetting sins); to be the visible sign in the world of the presence of Christ. We can be sure of their truth, and we can be united about them with our fellow-Christians, and especially fellow-members of our particular church, without fear of divisive controversy. But the trouble is that these truths still leave us with almost every question open about what is actually to be done. The moment you try to go on from them to any kind of criticism of an existing situation or proposals for action, that kind of assurance about the rightness of what you are saying has got to go. The diagnosis can be wrong, the ideas may be useless or even, if taken seriously, harmful. But there is no way of avoiding this risk. Silence and inaction do not avoid it either.

If we find ourselves considering the problem of the Church's job, or mission, in the modern world, asking self-critically whether it is being carried out, and if not why not and so forth, it is surely not because we fear that the job as scripturally stated is simply not being done at all. We can look at all Christian communions and see that the reign of God is being proclaimed and that Christ's presence is being shown forth in loving brotherhood and in the deliberate formal signs of the sacraments. What one fears is that this job is being hampered rather than furthered by an inheritance of all sorts of structures, activities, habits, priorities which are not conducive to it and ought to be reformed or even abolished: from that point on one should, of course, devote one's attention to one's own communion.

If it is true that a great deal of Roman Catholic structure, inherited by descent, is not conducive to the Church's job, scripturally understood (thus calling for dissent and reform), then this is

51

perhaps because these structures are not merely in some ways out of date but were actually designed for some different job, which we have mistakenly supposed to be the one assigned to us. I believe that a good deal of the shape and activity of the Church as we Roman Catholics have inherited it is the result of an uneasy attempt to combine the job of proclaiming the Kingdom and showing for the Son of Man in the world with the job of supplying people, and whole societies, with 'a religion': what they feel they want in the way of sacred activites, places, objects, feelings. This general complex of sacred activities performed in sacred places in which sacred objects are kept, tended by a sacred caste who are the real performers of the sacred actions, ordinary people sharing in them only, or at any rate chiefly, as recipients, is what I am calling 'religion'. The trouble with this, of course, is that the word, without quotes, of course, can be and constantly is used in other and completely Christian senses (e.g. James 1:27!). Perhaps the quotation marks can take care of this. In any case, I do not know what other label to use for that age-old human activity of organizing the sacred into special actions, places, persons and things so as to cater for people's desire to find it, and be thrilled to awe by it, when and where they want it, to have techniques available to them to draw on it or approach it when they feel they need to (with the corresponding possibility of keeping it at bay when not wanted); so I do not know how to avoid saying that redemption in Christ means, under one aspect, being cured of 'religion'; and hence that in taking on the job of supplying society (and, hopefully, all mankind) with 'religion' the church was taking on a job incompatible with its real job, and tending constantly to frustrate it.

Obviously there was never any conscious policy decision about this on anybody's part: it all just grew. But there it was: the community with the inevitably subversive and revolutionary job of proclaiming the Kingdom accepted the job of chaplain to society as it was, unregenerate power structure and all. The impact of this on the Church's job seems most sharply illustrated in the role of the Forces Chaplain in our society I would contend that from the military authorities' point of view, his job is to see that a number of men being used in an organized activity almost certainly incompatible with the Kingdom of God do not go hungry of 'religion', because that would be bad for their morale. If they are kept supplied with whatever they feel a need of in the way of the sacred, they will be a better fighting machine. He is also expected to use the authority of his membership of the sacred caste to exhort them to unquestioning military obedience. I cannot help seeing this as simply the ultimate, extreme form of the situation of the whole church in consenting to be the religion of an establishment.

It is not, however, an easy job to get rid of. How can you harden your heart and refuse to do whatever pastoral work is possible as military chaplain in even a manifestly, by any standards, unjust war? How can you simply turn on millions of people who expect you, and have been led to expect you, to supply them with a ritualized embodiment of the sacred, and tell them that your real job involves breaking it to them that the sacred, in the familiar, set-apart meaning of the word which is what they want, was shattered nineteen centuries ago when the veil was rent? It isn't only that what they want, which thousands on thousands of years of human beings have wanted, is to have a sacred caste with guaranteed supernatural powers to look after their 'religious' needs, and especially to provide them with a localized divine presence to dwell in a shrine in their neighbourhood temple; it is that they have been continually assured that that is, in fact, what the Christian church and eucharist were instituted to supply them with.

The job of supplying a folk-religion to those who want it, making available a pattern of sacred activities inside whatever sacred spaces society is willing to harbour within itself, is essentially a static, conformist, stabilizing role. Ironically, this sacred role which the church has allowed itself to accept (never totally, but all too extensively) for much of its history, is in an extreme and indeed caricatured form precisely the role it is officially allowed in most communist states. It is frighteningly like the kind of formula by which we nowadays try to convey to ourselves and others the real meaning of hell: a picture of God saying to the damned 'Very well, be what you have chosen to be.' On the other hand, the real job of proclaiming the Kingdom and being the sign in the world of the glorified Son of Man is essentially a revolutionary role, and would still be that in any socialist society with the Kingdom of God). It is also inescapably secular: human bodies are our temple, human lives lived in brotherhood and sonship are our sacrifice, sheer membership in the Son of Man our priesthood. Yes, we have the sign which embodies all this in a formal act of the whole community, and to call this action 'a sacrifice' and those who do the central specialized job in the performing of it 'priests' in a special sense does not have to be misleading language; it just happens to have become so. But if we are serious about the fact that we are here proclaiming the Lord's death until he come, and becoming one body, one Christ, by eating one loaf together, then we cannot, as we do, make a division between this and our mission to the world. We are here proclaiming, and committing ourselves to, a human world in which all are fed equally at the common table, none goes hungry: and this in virtue of our being one body with the Man who laid down his life to give life to men. This is not a static system of worship, of rendering a certain quota of due homage to an en-throned, emperor-like deity, by performing the set of actions prescribed as the sacred ceremonial of his court, and through that producing a static presence of him to be housed in our sacrally-protected shrine. That kind of sacral activity does not call for change in any social system which permits it, however contemptu-ously, to be practised. The reality of the Lord's Supper, on the other hand, is inescapably a proclamation of revolution. The people who do it declare themselves to have a mission to transform the world in the direction of that new humanity which they are identify-ing themselves with by eating the flesh of the Son of Man and drinking his blood. Such a mission, proclaimed in such a sacra-mental action, would naturally lead one to expect to find God's people normally welcoming and co-operating with revolutionary movements striving to achieve a social realization of that equally shared common table, that brotherhood. It would naturally lead one to expect that, faced with the violence with which men on all sides seek to realize their ends, God's Church would, if not parti-cipate in, yet instinctively excuse, and defend as relatively blame-less, the violence with which men seek to end exploitation and establish brotherhood, while condemning unreservedly, and draw-ing on itself the brunt of persecution from, the violence employed from the top to maintain exploitation and repress brotherhood.

The mission of being the sign in this world of the presence of the glorified Son of Man must, it seems from numerous passages in the gospels, be carried out in the same sort of terms as those obtaining for the Son of Man in his earthly ministry: not to be served but to serve, and to give His life for the many. We are indeed, these days, developing the habit of declaring ourselves the servant church. But to be *this* servant does not, in gospel terms, seem to mean drawing on the unjust wealth-structure of the world for ample funds with which to perform a limited, however generous, repertoire of relief works under the benign patronage of the power-structure whose activities continue to ensure that those relief works will be permanently necessary. It seems rather to mean so total an identification with the victims of the worldly situation, together with so subversive a proclamation of a revolution of God. coming to transform that situation, that the only possible response from the power structure must be arrest and execution.

I do not think that this job is compatible with the job of supplying institutionalized sacrality to people who want it. That is to say, I think that the two are in conflict: the church's man-given role of supplying 'religion' to a culture has been in conflict with its God-given role of proclaiming the Kingdom and being the sign of the Son of Man. What I do not mean by 'incompatible' is that the doing of the one has simply eliminated the doing of the other. Carrying out the God-given mission, the true task, has continued all the time, of course, and has constantly subverted the structure set up by the false task. But the false task has continually choked and overgrown the true. I believe that Vatican II was a huge upheaval in the direction of recovering consciousness of the true task and giving it priority. But it remains hampered by an unwillingness, a sheer inability, to abandon the false version of our job (and heaven help us, such abandonment means abandoning *people*: people who have, in a valid sense, a right to expect a continued supply of the 'religion' they have been encouraged to depend on). Perhaps the merciful wrath of God will do what we cannot: perhaps having had (too late as always) our deuteronomic reform, we shall learn the meaning of the servant in the violence of destruction and exile.

Mission

PAULINE WEBB

THE TROUBLE with Methodists is that they will insist on looking upon all the world as though it were their parish. It is not difficult to understand why. The great slogan of ecclesiastical disobedience which John Wesley hurled against the Anglican authorities who tried to confine him within appointed parochial boundaries has become the watchword of Methodist world mission: 'The world is my parish.'

The perils of this kind of parochial thinking, however wide its bounds may be set, is that it has come to contain within it the idea that mission begins with the church and ends with the church. Some still talk of 'mission campaigns', in which a local church, usually under imported leadership, directs a short-term assault on a neighbourhood, the results of which are measured in terms of the numbers who are then brought into closer touch with the church community. Our Division of Home Missions is still associated in many people's minds with the support of large mission halls, which, though they were originally built as churches in disguise in an attempt to attract the concert-going crowds, have now for the most part become openly ecclesiastical, centres of a gathered congregation. Our world mission is recognized in red spots on a globe-shaped missionary box, which mark those places where Methodism has planted its churches overseas. So, although the idea of mission is deep implanted in the Methodist soul, and it is often claimed that one cannot be a member of the Methodist Church without being by that very fact committed to her mission to the world (every Methodist is expected, for example, to support 'Missions' at home and overseas as part of his Church commitment), one wonders on what theological presuppositions this zeal for mission rests. How far have we Methodists yet begun to grasp the overwhelming implications of the truth that the mission is not our initiative but God's activity, in which the Church is called to participate not for her own sake but for the sake of the world which He loves, not because it is our parish but because it is His Kingdom?

There is no doubt, however, about the over-riding motive for mission that drove the Wesleys. It is sounded repeatedly in the doctrinal text-book of the early Methodists, the hymns of Charles Wesley. Their gospel was the good news of a universal Saviour, a universality which Methodists sang out emphatically, drowning the protests of any would-be Calvinists. 'For all, for all,' Charles sings again and again in a phrase that is more than a couple of useful iambic feet to fill out a line of verse. For the Wesleys it is the rhythmic beat of their mandate for mission, a motto expounded more fully by John in his sermon on Assurance—'All men can be saved; all men can know that they are saved; all men can be saved to the uttermost.' Conversion, to the early Methodists, meant not only a turning to Christ, but also a turning to all classes and conditions of men in a passionate concern for their souls' welfare. Across the pages of Wesley's Journal jostle courtiers and coal-miners, statesman and servants, and among his preachers were those whom Laurence Sterne described contemptuously as 'illiterate mechanics, more fitted to make a pulpit than to get into one', a gibe to which Wesley proudly retorted, 'In the one thing they profess to know, they are not ignorant men. I trust there is not one of them who is not able to go through such an examination in substantial, practical, experimental divinity as few of our graduates from Holy Orders even in the University are able to do.'[1]

This substantial, practical, experimental theology was in Wesley's concept of mission expressed not solely in the preaching of what he somewhat decisively called 'gospel sermons'. Wesley had little time for ranters, who with 'neither sense nor grace bawl out some-thing about Christ or his blood or justification by faith.... We know no gospel without salvation from sin.' So with the message of the Saviour he offered a programme of reform. The mission of Methodism was, he declared, 'to spread scriptural holiness through-out the land' and though an excessive individualism marked the preaching of many early Methodists, it was Wesley's oft-repeated conviction that 'Christianity is essentially a social religion: and to turn it into a solitary one is to destroy it.... Our Lord is so far from directing us to break off all commerce with the world that without it, according to his account of Christianity, we cannot be

Christians at all.'[2] So he urged the people called Methodists to make their daily employment a sacrifice to God, to buy and sell, to eat and drink to His glory. It does not seem incongruous, then, to find among the relics of a man who vowed that he had nothing to do but save souls, an electrical invention for curing rheumatism as part of his mission to their bodies too. Nor is it out of character that a man avowedly Tory in politics should leave as his last letter a clarion call in defence of the equal rights of all men. It is to Wilberforce that he writes, urging him in the struggle against the 'execrable villainy' of the slave-trade.

Wesley's own close knowledge of what he called the 'vilest slavery that ever saw the sun, American slavery', came from a long contact with that continent and a strategy of mobility which had sent the Methodist preachers riding out with the frontiersmen in their great drive westward. Wherever men were on the move, Methodists must move with them and no ecclesiastical structure could be permitted to restrict Wesley and his preachers in their pioneer role. The travelling preachers were sent where the action was—'no road was too boggy, no weather too inclement, no ford too swollen, no community too degraded, no mob too violent, no privation too severe . . .' writes one biographer of these early travelling preachers. To those who wanted at all costs to preserve the *status quo*, these men pushing out into new areas of life and territory were seen to be a social threat. When five or six thousand miners in Bristol stopped in their tracks on their way to work to listen to an open-air preacher, the *Gentleman's Magazine* reported in alarm: 'If one man can thus detain the vulgar from their daily labour, what a loss this may bring to the public. For my part I shall expect to hear of a prodigious rise in the price of coal about the city of Bristol if this gentleman proceeds with his charitable lectures to the colliers of Kingswood.' The fears were well-founded, for it was in many of those early Methodist groups that working men first discovered their own human dignity, and those whose tongues had first been loosened to proclaim good news about God eventually became articulate too in demanding the rights of men. It is no coincidence that five of the six Tolpuddle Martyrs were Methodists, even though those who pioneered the mission among them probably never realized the full implications of this gospel of liberty. It was this same sense of mission that determined Wesley's action. He worked out the theology afterwards—which is perhaps what a pilgrim theology such as his must always be prepared to do.

But what became of this pilgrim theology when the people called Methodists passed out of their pioneer era into what has been called their 'mahogany age'? Through well-learned lessons of thrift, prudence and piety, Methodist societies were becoming, by the time of Wesley's death, predominantly middle class. The visible sign of their presence among men within the second century of their history became more often than not the large buildings, so inappropriately called 'chapels', which rivalled in size if not in magnificence the local parish church. Here, in edifices which, it has been pointed out, looked uncommonly like railway termini, the Methodist people seemed to have arrived at their destination. Such 'missions' as still went on were sporadic campaigns for survival, which served to bring others in to the established centre. Attempts to break out from the rigidity which institutionalism imposed upon what once had been movement, resulted in fragmentation, and the second half of the nineteenth century finds a broken Methodism more conscious perhaps of the need for an ecclesiology than for a theology of mission. Now the system and obedience to it became all important. 'Methodism is as much opposed to democracy as to sin', declared Jabez Bunting, the mid-century Methodist autocrat.

Yet the lure of the frontiers remained and throughout the nineteenth century the appeal of mission overseas became more and more clamant in Methodist ears. At the beginning of the century the fiery little Welshman Thomas Coke had ignited a flame of missionary fervour which went on shooting out sparks (often emigrant laymen and women in the first instance) into new areas of Methodist influence right across the world, until the map of the Methodist Church began to bear a more than coincidental resemblance to the map of the British Empire.

This was the century for works of charity, but there were heard too the voices of those prophets who began to see that charity could be regarded as only a temporary substitute for justice. There were those who hoped that such justice would come about as the result of individual integrity and personal concern as R. S. Inglis has illustrated.[3] He quotes Hugh Price Hughes, one of the most ardent Methodist advocates of social reform, as writing in the *Methodist Times* 'In answer to the employer's question: "What must I do to be saved?", might we not say, "Believe in the Lord Christ Jesus and adjust your wages sheet." ' There were other prophets who took much further the implications of Hughes' own declaration that 'Jesus Christ came into this world to save human society as well as to save individuals. Indeed, you cannot effectively save one without saving the other.' 'I would not be content with appeals that sought rather to palliate existing evils by charitable help,' wrote Scott Lidgett, who was the founder of the Bermondsey Settlement, 'than radically to reconstruct the existing organisation of society on the basis of righteousness and the comradeship of brotherly love.'[4]

The present century began with an American Methodist layman, John R. Mott,[5] expressing the missionary motive of the whole ecumenical movement as he declared its aim as being 'The evangelisation of all the world in this generation'. Perhaps the most significant evidence of the great change that has come about in our understanding of mission during this twentieth century is to be seen in the fact that at a recent Overseas Consultation, to which Methodist leaders from all parts of the world came, it was suggested that the contemporary equivalent of that slogan should be, 'A fully human life for all humanity'.

In his book *The Names of Jesus*, Dr J. Vincent Taylor, a twentieth-century Methodist theologian, has described Christology as 'the despairing attempt of theologians to keep pace with the Church's apprehension of Christ'. 'Every age', he writes, 'will know better who Christ is.' In this age the Christ who seems to be breaking in upon His Church is the Christ who is the Son of Man, the Son of David, the Son of God.

He is the Son of Man, whose coming the Church celebrates. Perhaps we still have not grasped firmly enough the reality of the humanity of Jesus. So often the mission as expressed by the Church has almost seemed to rob those who responded to it of the full quality of their own humanity. The stereotype of expected Christian behaviour and patterns of Church life have been stamped upon them so rapidly that it has almost obliterated that original individuality which is God's unique gift to every son of man. Yet we live in an age today where men yearn above all else to explore in all its fullness the potentiality of human personality. The 'little boxes made of ticky-tacky' into which, as Pete Seeger sings, our technological society compresses us, are as coffins against which our living souls beat out for release. We do not want to be 'all just the same', and yet we are terrified of our differences. We want to claim our right to be independent of each other, and yet we become ever more aware of our inevitable interdependence. We long to be fully human and yet all the advances in our human condition in medicine and machinery, in social structures and political systems, seem to threaten progressive dehumanization.

What does it mean, then, in this kind of a world, to confess that Christ is the Son of Man, the One who is present in every humanizing event, who sets men free to be themselves and to love one another? Mission means to share in those events, to take part in all that makes for man's full humanity, working in partnership with all who are striving to bring greater dignity to human living, to humanize the structures of human society, to secure for all the full attainment of their human rights. It means sharing in the search for new forms of community which will break down the barriers behind which we hide from one another. It means discovering the possibility of a unity of mankind which dares to contain within it the rich diversity of the human family. In this kind of community we Christians must be as ready to listen as to speak, to receive as to give, to learn as to teach, for in every person and his uniqueness we learn more of the Son of Man in whom all our perfected humanity is revealed.

Yet if we are to explore fully all that is implied by this participation in the humanizing work of the Son of Man, we need to understand much more deeply what was meant by those who hailed him as Son of David, the Messiah of Jewish hopes, the one in whom the promises of God were fulfilled and the Kingdom of God had come. We have often sounded as though the coming of the Kingdom of God depended on our bringing it in, as though the Church were its only embassy in a foreign territory. We have hardly yet begun to explore the full implications of the New Testament teaching that he is already the Lord, the one into whose hands the kingdoms of this world are given and to whose rule all human rulers are subject. He rules not only over the Church, but over the world, and his Church is called not only to be the visible demonstration to men of what that rule means, but also to be among the active agents realizing that rule among all men. So Christians recognize his reign over all the power structures of the world, and if they would truly follow their Lord they must follow him there in the places where decisions are made and government operates.

For many years now, Methodism has acknowledged the concept of citizenship as one expression of mission. It has more than a mere change of name when, in 1950, what had formerly been the Temperance and Moral Welfare Department became known as the Christian Citizenship Department and later the Division of Social Responsibility. Since that time social and political questions on a variety of subjects have come under the scrutiny of committees which, because of their specialist ability and competence, have won the confidence of the Church as it seeks to help people towards a Christian judgement on controversial and contemporary issues. But by its very structure, this Division inevitably operates from within the Church, scrutinizing the political councils from outside, whilst full political involvement is left to individuals, whose political activity still tends to be regarded as an extra-Church affair, again often suspected as 'eccentric' since it is centred in the world rather than the Church. We need to take much more seriously the political expressions of the ministry of the people of God.

It seems as though the closing quarter of this century is going to make a change in emphasis in the Church's mission from the concern for charity on a world scale to a much more political concept of international economic and social justice, expressed in World Council of Churches' documents which describe as priority situations for mission today the centres of power, the revolutionary movements, the universities, the new urban areas, which are so radically changing the structures of modern society.

Yet, even this new emphasis on political involvement in citizenship could become a distorted one, unless the concepts of Christ, Son of Man and Son of David, are held together in tension with the concepts of Christ, Son of God, whose final victory the Church confidently anticipates. We know he is present in the world, but we know too that wherever he is present the demons gather, and we join in the struggle against the principalities and powers which so often seem to usurp his rule. Yet to realise that the one who rules the earth is also the one seated on the throne of the universe reduces all our human activity and apprehensions to their true diminutive dimensions. To acknowledge his eternal reign is to relativize all our temporal systems so that nothing is granted eternal significance save Christ alone. All of our ecclesiastical structures must be seen as provisional and open to change. It is no conicidence that it has been those engaged in the frontiers of mission who have become most aware of the inhibitions of the institutional Church. 'Mobilising the people of God for mission today', states a World Council of Churches' Report, calling for a new stance in Church life, 'means releasing them from structures that inhibit them in the Church and enabling them to open out in much more flexible ways to the world in which they live. The question to be asked', goes on the Report, 'is not "Have we the right structures for mission?" but "Are we totally structured for mission?".'

To be totally structured for mission would mean that the people called Methodists would become again a pilgrim people giving ourselves to the world, not as a parish where we may gather all safely in, but as the Kingdom in which our Lord calls us to celebrate his coming, to demonstrate his rule, to anticipate his victory as we joyfully worship, work and wait until he come and all things are finally consummated in him.

NOTES

[1] See *Wesley's Journal.*

[2] See *Wesley's Journal.*

[3] R. S. Inglis, *Churches and the Working Classes in Victorian England* (Routledge and Kegan Paul).

[4] For Scott Lidgett's life, see the Symposium, *Scott Lidgett* (Epworth).

[5] *John R. Mott—Layman Extraordinary*: A Symposium (Hodder).

4

WORSHIP AND SPIRITUALITY

John Coventry and Gordon S. Wakefield

Roman Catholic Worship and Spirituality

JOHN COVENTRY

THE ROMAN CATHOLIC Church is in the middle of digest-
ing something of a revolution in worship. Hence it must be a
fairly tentative and subjective task for anyone to try to describe
and comment on Roman Catholic spirituality at this precise
moment. Someone else's impressions could be quite different. In
any case, where are anyone's impressions drawn from? Roman
Catholicism has never been quite the same in England, Scotland
and Ireland—to say nothing of other European countries and four
other continents. It is not possible in these pages to do more than
attempt to survey the local scene.

The Tridentine services in Latin—not only for Mass, but for
baptism, confirmation, penitential absolution, weddings and
funerals—were austere, intellectual, majestic, remote, impersonal:
they were classically beautiful (when done properly!). This was a
sacralized liturgy, conducted by a sacral caste in sacral robes and
settings, witnessed by worshippers from afar. It had its great point
in the supposedly Christian lands of the west where the Church
and the world had become the same people, as a witness to the
holiness of God and the primacy of God's activity over man's.
The worship of God stood apart, as what was holy and not everyday, from the lives of ordinary Christian people: for they were also
the world, the secular. A minority of educated Catholics followed
the Mass in their own missals, and liked Vespers or Compline. They
treasured the silence of the Canon and the contemplative climate of
the whole liturgy. (This is what the Latin Mass Society mourns.) A
wider group of the devout had their own devotional methods for
interior involvement in the Mass, which could include the rosary.
The rest were simply there.

One result of this austered liturgy, involving little or no lay
participation, was that the personal piety and emotional needs of
believers needed outlet and found expression in a proliferation

Dissent and Descent

of non-liturgical services and 'devotions': Benediction and processions of the Blessed Sacrament, with hymns, banners, brass bands, white-frocked girls strewing rose petals; flowers galore, on the altar and in the church; candles as symbols of prayer burning all day; Stations of the Cross; litanies, novenas, devotions to the Sacred Heart; and of course the deeply felt and pervasive devotion to Our Lady. Of this latter devotion one cannot write adequately in a few words; one cannot write meaningfully of what must first be part of Christian experience to have meaning. Criticisms that devotion to Our Lady somehow deflected worship from God have never made the slightest sense to Catholic experience; this always found her a central way of experiencing or being aware of God. In default of fuller treatment, one may perhaps simply leave the suggestion that devotion to Our Lady as it has flourished in Catholicism must be seen together with, and not apart from, the 'sacralized' liturgy.

Roman Catholicism believes profoundly in our expressing our faith in every human way, and has never felt much need to apologize for 'simple people' doing so in ways that seem appropriate to them, even if they seem sugary, gaudy, sentimental, to the more educated and fastidious. Even if they seem superstitious, one must be very careful not to equate the outward expression with the faith that is being expressed. The latin races never allowed the liturgy itself to remain wholly austere and remote: they brought their violins, chickens and vines into church; they found (and still find) our Anglo-Saxon Catholicism extremely dull. One of the sad results of the Reformation for English Catholicism was the death of its native customs and the subsequent importation of 'devotions' from abroad.

The current revolution, then, is basically a reversal—a very sudden reversal—of these two trends: an austered liturgy, devotional expression in extra-liturgical ways. It is therefore much more far-reaching than a change from Latin to English. The 'new Mass', like the new baptismal and other rites, is meant to involve the whole congregation as fully as possible throughout. It is an exercise in communication, of celebrant with people and of people with each other. It expresses and deepens a sense of community: indeed, it can create a sense of community, for instance in a concelebration or when celebrated in a private house for those living in the street or

68

immediate area. Priest and people enter it together in the exchanges of the penitential rite. Different members of the congregation read the lessons from Scripture and involve the whole gathering in the responsorial psalm. The priest's homily becomes more like a meditation out loud on what has just been heard; occasionally others will speak their own thoughts. The intercessions are not meant to be formalized prayers, but more spontaneous prayers geared to current needs; members of the congregation sometimes contribute. An offertory procession will follow. Singing at this and other places becomes an integral part of the liturgy, not something done by the people while the clergy get on with their liturgical functions; and only rarely now is it a matter of the many listening to the concert performance of a few. All respond to the celebrant's Eucharistic Prayer. All prepare with him for Holy Communion, by the Our Father, by exchanging the kiss of peace, and by singing or reciting 'Lamb of God'. If there is a Communion hymn, it should be sung while people are receiving.

The frequent reception of Holy Communion, and its administration to quite young children, have become customary over the last sixty years since Pius X. Both have been most rich and fruitful experiences of Catholic life. Many laity are virtually daily communicants. They used to manage simply by getting up early. Now the relaxation of the rigid fasting rules, and the introduction of midday and evening Masses, have helped and encouraged them. The involvement of the congregation in the Mass throughout, leads more and more towards people taking it for granted that they go to Mass, not only to give honour and glory to God, but to receive Communion—or, rather, that they do the former most by doing the latter. Communion becomes less a private meeting with Our Lord, more a corporate act, deepening the unity of all who share in it.

Conversely, as the liturgy increasingly caters for the whole man and satisfies his devotional and personal needs, the extra-liturgical exercises of piety begin at once to fade away. It is hardly an exaggeration to say that some have died overnight. Devotional evening services wither; the statues, candles, flowers, begin to vanish; the once familiar scent of incense lingers only around solemn celebrations in large churches. Now that most priests recite the Divine Office in English, the new forms of Morning and Evening Prayer can make excellent extra-sacramental services of worship of a more contemplative kind. Whereas verve had previously to be expressed outside the liturgy, now the guitar comes into it. Some few are experimenting with liturgical dancing (the oldest form of religious expression). The new *missa normativa* begins to be seen as a general structure, rather than as a set piece, and in house Masses, school Masses, group Masses, a good deal of improvisation takes place: the celebration is found 'meaningful' in so far as those present combine to express themselves in it. If priests are involved, over and above the presiding celebrant, they less and less feel any need to be distinguishable in any way from the general community.

Something similar is happening to Confession. For long it was an essentially private sacrament, a personal exercise with, preferably, anonymity on both sides; a rare event for any real sinners; a weekly or fortnightly personal discipline for the devout, especially if they were frequent communicants. Today a 'private sacrament' is felt to be something of a contradiction in terms. Sin and forgiveness both come to be measured in terms of one's fellow men. The Church is seen to be a reconciling community through and through, expressing Christ's forgiveness in a whole spectrum of shared activity, from the penitential rite at the beginning of every Mass to a more carefully prepared Liturgy of Penance, perhaps during Lent, possibly in an all-night vigil. Within such a spectrum there is room for, and there is much profit in, a personal stock-taking and a personal ecceptance of Christ's forgiveness. But this tends to be at rarer intervals, and not necessarily in a 'confessional' environment: a young person will come to talk in an exploratory way about what they then and there find to be important in life, and will quite simply ask for sacramental absolution at the end.

In a number of parishes things are at the moment neither one thing nor the other. Rather than being quite clear about the meaning of the new liturgy and of what they are trying to do, priest and people are often feeling their way. At one extreme one may find a parish priest somewhat mechanically and unhappily following a new set of directions that have come to him wholly from outside, trying perhaps to convey the old atmosphere through new words and gestures. In another parish the whole thing will have come alive with vitality and warmth; it will have a certain informality and a relaxed atmosphere which show that real communication and personal relationships have taken the place of a series of rather formal tableaux added disjointedly to one another.

There is a good deal of malaise about the English of the formal and oft-repeated liturgical prayers. The rhetorical cadences of Latin had a dignity and solemnity that conveyed the momentous nature of the occasion (when they were intelligently recited!). The English attempts to be direct, simple, drawn from current usage, avoiding any stylized language that would sound artificial; the result is undistinguished, banal. Perhaps the root of the trouble is that the recurring formulas and Eucharistic Prayers are translations from Latin and not original compositions in English; hence they compare unfavourably with some modern Anglican and Methodist texts.

The Tridentine liturgy of the Mass had large areas of quiet. Now there seems to be an uninterrupted torrent of sound, of undigested words. Three bible readings, often very diverse, follow each other somewhat breathlessly and the celebrant is hard put to it to extract from them any single and connected thread of thought, let alone one that meets any real needs of the people. It is hardly traditional in Roman Catholicism to suppose that the words of Scripture will have some quasi-automatic effect of their own! The short time of silence after Communion is very welcome, but it comes only at the end; there is need of some pools of silence all through.

The new eucharistic liturgy is an exercise in communication throughout, and so makes very great demands on the actual use of the voice by the celebrant (and the readers). It presupposes a professional training he will not have had, to sustain life, interest, variety, without imposing his own personality. Instead, one hears the same voice with the same cadences going on and on. . . .

More profoundly, some are disturbed by the basic spiritual attitude implied in such a liturgy. There are murmurs about vulgarization, about the absence of any sense of awe and mystery. Whatever its shortcomings, the Tridentine Mass expressed the presence of the divine reality in our midst, the worship of the angels brought down to earth, or the raising up of the human community into the communion of saints gathered round the heavenly altar where the Lamb lies eternally, both victorious and slain. Are we not in danger of dimming the sense of God's action by making such a fuss about our own? Yet, over against this it must be said that so many find the celebration meaningful in a totally new way: it has come alive for them; it is something in which they can so much more easily involve their children; ordinary life flows into the eucharistic liturgy; in turn, it reaches out to other sacramental rites, to private prayers and to prayers in the home.

At risk of caricaturing, one might say that in medieval and renaissance times it was thought to be proper to priests and members of religious orders to have a personal spiritual life. The *Spiritual Exercises* of Ignatius of Loyola in the latter part of the sixteenth century, and the *Introduction to the Devout Life* of Francis de Sales in the first half of the seventeenth, were among the chief instruments in launching a movement of lay spirituality. Catholicism sees the Christian life as a spectrum extending from the most withdrawn and contemplative vocation, through the active religious orders, to the committed 'lay apostle'. God calls different people differently, giving different gifts, and there can be no standard blend of contemplation and action that can be called 'the' Christian life. In every form of Christian life there is some blend of these elements, but the emphasis will vary. It is only the whole Church that can even try to mirror and exemplify the life of Christ's Spirit in man. Spirituality for the laity as it developed in Catholicism through retreats and writings on prayer was essentially an extension to at any rate the more educated laity of the practices of meditation or contemplation, and of self-assessment, that were part of the daily rule of life in religious orders. Writers like de Caussade and others helped them to find God in their daily occupations, rather than by temporary withdrawal from them.

It seems fairly certain that historians will come to see the main development of Catholicism in the twentieth century as the progressive involvement of the laity in the apostolate or mission of the Church. This has been backed by an increasing search by such committed lay people for a personal life of meditative prayer, either on their own with the help of retreats and counsellors and books, or in groups which share prayerful reflection on passages of Scripture. A very central feature of Catholic life and experience has been that the reserved Sacrament in the church has truly been the effective sign of Christ's presence in our midst, and the focus of piety. Many a Catholic 'pops in for a visit' for a few minutes, or finds it possible to spend a longer time of silence and contemplation in the stillness of the church before the Lord. Protestant critics of Reservation have tended (naturally enough) to focus on 'the cultus' and to overlook what was more profound and less obtrusive. One wonders whether the new corporateness that is being experienced in the liturgy will tend to diminish this long-standing but more private feature of Catholic spirituality. It could just as well make the need for it more keenly felt. It is too early to say.

Be that as it may, a quite new phenomenon is taking hold in the Roman Catholic Church—the charismatic prayer group. Much has been written on this, and it is difficult if not impossible to assess its meaning or value in a page or two. The phenomenon, if that is an allowable designation, neither originated in Catholicism, nor has it appeared in the Roman Catholic more than in other established Churches, except perhaps in America. Not by the wildest stretch of the imagination could it yet be called a characteristic feature of Roman Catholic life and spirituality as a whole. Rather, what has been found remarkable is that it could have found a place in Roman Catholicism at all. It is this fact that calls for some effort at interpretation.

In the Pentecostalist Churches group prayer is fed by a fundamentalist reliance on the Bible, and is strongly emotional and demonstrative in its expression. It often appears to be the cry of those who are dispossessed in this life, finding relief and hope in an eschatological future. Classical pentecostalism has not shown interest in solving the problems that confront society, though there are signs of its beginning to move in this direction; it has been a gospel of personal salvation through experience of, and reception of, the Spirit. Though no doubt influenced by pentecostalism of this kind, charismatic prayer in the traditional Churches appears to have other origins, to meet other needs, and in general to take much quieter forms. What is interesting in Catholicism is that group prayer is catching on precisely among the same sort of people who earlier in the century were reading the mystical and ascetical writers and making serious efforts to develop the practice of private mental prayer in their own lives. Both laity and members of religious orders, after battling perhaps for some years in aridity at the prie-dieu before an absent God, begin to discover the reality and the nearness of God's presence in their midst, when they sit in a quiet circle, voicing occasionally their aspirations and their helplessness.

73

Younger people, who would a generation ago have entered the experience of mental prayer at the thinking-things-out stage (meditation in the narrower sense of the term), now like to do their thinking out together in a group; they reason it out with God; they talk to God rather than to each other; there is much of praise in their prayer; but they find they can only do this with others in a group, aware of each other, assisting each other in their talking to God, only finding God present in a group. In revolt to a greater or lesser extent against the materialism of the culture they have inherited, they search for a spirituality and know that it can only be found in people. God dwells and is at work in the heart of man, not in physical interventions 'out there' in nature.

If this is a reasonably accurate description of how group prayer is experienced, then one cannot help noting that it fits very well into what has been a traditionally catholic (in the broadest sense) view of the Church. It has been a protestant emphasis that God acts upon the individual through the words of Scripture; whereas catholic theology and catholic 'sense' in general has wanted to stress that the Church in Christ's Body, that the reality of his presence and action is to be found first within the living community itself, and that Scripture only takes on meaning within a living tradition which it constantly forms. For this reason Catholicism has always been more corporate and therefore more sacramental.

On the other hand, the power to pray, and to be aware of God's activity in the *smaller* group, exactly echoes what evangelicals have all along been repeating about the local Church. This is perhaps no more than a sidelight on a fact that is gaining increasing recognition—the ecumenical value of the charismatic prayer movement. The wider ground and context for this is the discovery of the Spirit in humanity as such, with the result that almost by definition the group, or the movement, knows no barriers, denominational or of any other kind.

Finally, in the present context of Roman Catholic worship and spirituality, one cannot help noticing that the emergence of charismatic prayer groups in Roman Catholicism coincides almost to the day with the introduction of the new liturgy of the Mass. Is it perhaps part of the explanation of what is going on that the silent and contemplative elements of the Tridentine Mass, now as it were banished from the liturgy, are finding this alternative outlet? If so, there would seem to be no need to be apprehensive of any conflict or tug-of-war between the two forms of prayer. There is no reason why one should not feed the other. And various assessments of the charismatic movement that have been made by Roman Catholic and other authorities are agreed that, so far from the groups tending to become an alternative to the Church, this experience of prayer attaches people more firmly to the life of their own historic traditions. And it makes them peaceable: the communion and unity they experience with their fellow Christians 'in the Spirit' is big enough and deep enough to sustain disagreements and tensions. It is interior and in a sense substantial, making differences seem more outward and secondary, even trivial. This is the basic reason for its ecumenical force.

It would no doubt be of interest to other Christians to have some indication of the type or types of Christian that Roman Catholic spirituality produces. But this is an extremely difficult task to perform for a number of reasons. First, as with national characteristics which you assume as natural rather than view objectively, it is far easier for others to observe and give fair portraits of the distinguishing features. Secondly, because Roman Catholicism is more international than Reformation traditions. Thirdly, because it is in a state of particularly rapid change.

All western Churches have, of course, spread to Asia and Africa through missionary enterprise, and have founded Asian and African forms of their traditions; but it may be doubted whether in these continents wholly de-Europeanized and truly indigenous forms of Christianity have yet found their self-expression. In saying that Roman Catholicism is more international, I wish firstly to note that it remained established (and was exported) in all the European traditions, including for instance those of Slav peoples; and these are very different from each other. Secondly, it is all too often forgotten that Eastern Christianity exists within Catholicism in the Uniate Churches. Hence I venture to suggest that it is part of Catholicism to expect and to accept a great diversity of 'Christian types'. A Roman Catholic in Britain, encountering in the ecumenical scene mainly Churches of British tradition, and even origin, will often feel that Anglo-Saxon cultural attitudes are in some way assumed as the vehicle of Christian expression—or even regarded as the norm by which other forms of expression are to be judged!

On the other hand, Roman Catholic priests the world over were, until very recently, formed in the same mould of scholastic philosophy and theology, and used the same Latin text-books. The cultural diversity of peoples was held together firmly by a sort of super-culture that was that of no actual nation, yet imposed clearly definable patterns of thinking of its own. There were two great and allied forces at work in high scholasticism: the concept of law; and a deductive type of systematic thinking in clearly defined concepts. The teaching of Christian doctrine in Roman Catholicism characteristically started from abstract and even technical thought-systems, adducing Scripture by way of illustration; its moral teaching sought to proceed similarly by way of deduction from and application of fixed rules, after the manner of codified law. Both processes led to a sense of clarity, fixity, assurance, uniformity. Other Christians have found Roman Catholics 'legalistic'. Though in this country this owes something to the 'RC system', it also owes a good deal to Anglo-Saxon literalness on the part of Roman Catholics. One finds that the Latin peoples (perhaps the peoples who came under the influence of the Code Napolèon) have a very, very different attitude to law. Two great statues stand in Rome of Peter holding the keys to himself, and Paul pointing out into the distance: this used to be interpreted as meaning, 'We make the laws: you keep them!' The English and the Germans have tended to do so....

Be that as it may, since long before the Second Vatican Council forces were at work to dismantle 'the system' as new thrusts of insight made themselves felt. A sense of history overtook that of eternal truth. Parallel with the liturgical revival has gone a biblical renewal that starts from Scripture and seeks to understand its intrinsic thought patterns and non-hellenic modes of expression for their own sake. Roman Catholic spirituality today is increasingly fed by, not so much a verse by verse listening to the Bible, as an attempt to grasp the main themes of biblical thought as they develop in the Old Testament and come to fullness of realization and expression in the New. At the same time, philosophical pluralism has increasingly broken into the doctrinal and systematic field. One of the most radical changes introduced by Paul VI will, surely, come in time to be seen as that of switching from the idea of training Catholic priests by a centrally guided system, to embracing pluriformity and encouraging the education of priests within the cultural and academic traditions of their own countries. Meanwhile Roman Catholics are alternately excited, sometimes headily excited, by a sense of discovery and opportunity, or dismayed and disturbed by the apparent dissolution of their accepted framework. The challenge that faced 'the fathers' of the Council, from their first Constitution on the Liturgy onwards to the end, was that of maintaining unity in diversity. The challenge that faces Roman Catholicism today is precisely the same. It is the challenge that faces Anglican and Protestant Churches in their struggle for unity: only, they are starting from the other end.

Perhaps we have strayed a bit far afield from the specific topic of Roman Catholics worship and spirituality. But this broader background is meant as a rough guide to others in interpreting what they may find in Catholicism today. Against it, two final sketches may briefly be attempted.

Roman Catholics are instructed, even drilled, in some basic rules: Sunday Mass; Easter Duties, i.e. Confession and Communion at least yearly around Easter time. The purpose is to instil a basic sense that it is man's duty to worship God, his Creator and Redeemer, and that if he does not do even that much a man is seriously turning away from God. Those of more good will find it a great support and help to have a rule about it, and they then make positive efforts to make their worship as meaningful as possible. Those whose Christian belief has penetrated less deep will be more inclined to keep at least some contact with the Church's worship, and their priests have some contact with them. The Roman Catholic Church is in this way able to experience itself, and is sometimes seen by others, as the Church for sinners. The fact that it is a normal rule for all to go to Confession from time to time (Confessions are particularly 'heavy' at Christmas and Easter) enables many to feel that the Church always has a welcome for them, and helps them to make fresh starts.

But perhaps the most characteristic thing about Catholicism is its sacramental sense. The Catholic does not feel himself primarily or directly confronted by Scripture as the medium of his meeting with God. He has a strong sense of the Church as the living Body of Christ into which he has been baptized; of Christ teaching in the Church, which preaches and meditates on the faith of the apostles as it is witnessed in the New Testament; of Christ forgiving and sanctifying in the sacraments; of Christ's love of the Father gathering all into itself in the Eucharist; of the continuing prayer of the Spirit in the Church into which we have only to join. The sacraments bring the realities of heaven into his own life, and gather all his world into God's service. The communion of saints is a real family to which he belongs, and it is from within this family sense that he prays for the dead or venerates Our Lady and the Saints. (The invocation in the Hail Mary, 'pray for us sinners', does not mean 'God is too remote so I pray to you instead'; but, 'I don't feel too confident about the value of my prayers, so please pray at my side and in my place'. The Blessed Sacrament in the tabernacle ensures that God is never remote.) Material symbols and external actions all help to support and deepen the sense of 'mystery', of divine reality present and active in our midst, of Christ sanctifying the whole life of man and being Lord of all creation. The danger of sacramentalism is that it can lead to a religion of externals, a religion of the flesh that has lost the Spirit. Its strength is that it involves the whole man and his world; he expects to enjoy his religion and to find it colourful. Sacramentalism enables him to take a positive and optimistic view of the good things God has created. He has a sense that in Christ God has redeemed, not just the inner soul of men, but the world.

Methodist Spirituality and Worship

GORDON S. WAKEFIELD

IT IS NOW apparent that the true genius of Methodism lay in its reconciliation of spontaneity with order, enthusiasm with an unwavering credal orthodoxy, and the needs of the working classes of the first Industrial and Agrarian revolutions with the tradition of 'the great Church'. This seems to have been due to the phenomenon of an eighteenth-century folk-movement led by Oxford dons, who, in addition to their solid Prayer Book Anglicanism, were susceptible to spiritualities other than their own.

Methodism was thus delivered from fanaticism, heterodoxy and bigotry. A Yorkshire Methodist in 1798, while sharing the common anti-Jesuit prejudices of Englishmen and Protestants in his day, could none the less write admiringly of the devotion of Ignatius Loyola and Francis Xavier, while a few years later, a young itinerant preacher was eager to emulate Gregory Lopez, a sixteenth-century Spanish recluse in Mexico, who testified that his every breath was prayer.

Methodism has never been a liturgical communion, in the Orthodox, Catholic, or Anglican sense. Its basic rite was that of the Book of Common Prayer, 1662, though this was rarely the principal service of the Lord's Day. Catholics who have heard rumours that the Wesleys were frequent communicants themselves, and presided at crowded Eucharists at a time when the Church of England as a whole was mostly content with Morning Prayer, Litany and Ante-Communion, may wonder why the sacramental revival was not maintained. The explanation is partly that Wesleyan Methodism, after Wesley's death, was reluctant to compete with the Established Church to which it professed great loyalty, and rather hoped that its members might communicate at their parish altars. We must also reckon with the fact that before the Oxford Movement—and perhaps indeed after it—the Englishman revered the Lord's institution, and subscribed to it occasionally, but was not

79

by nature a frequent communicant; and this despite a wealth of devotional writing, Anglican, Puritan and Methodist. The Methodist was no different from most of his Protestant fellow-countrymen. The Oxford Movement itself by its abhorrence of Methodism, as well as by the suspicions of a drift to Rome, which it aroused, did not encourage Methodist fidelity to the doctrines of the Wesley *Hymns on the Lord's Supper.*

There is a further reason. The life of the Methodist Societies—as the local churches were called—was often directed towards inducing the experience called conversion. This not only involved the attempt to reform notorious evil-doers, the local drunkards, wife-beaters and blasphemers, but the bringing of all those in a state of nature, however outwardly blameless, into a state of grace. Like some of the seventeenth-century Puritans, Methodists tended to believe that everyone should undergo the emotional trauma of self despair through consciousness of sin and self restoration through assurance of pardon. So much effort might be concentrated on this that Wesley's own insistence on holiness was ignored, or else made the *raison d'être* of a second crisis of personality as the wayfaring believer was in a moment transported into perfect love. This evangelical excitement, which some Methodists thus regarded as the proper mood of their Christianity, was not conducive to an ordered sacramental life; there were times when the sacraments themselves, as in Wesley's day, were scenes of great fervour and vocal enthusiasm, 'converting' as well as 'confirming' the ordinances.

Morning Prayer was used in some Wesleyan Chapels from their foundation, and still hangs on in a very few. It was often followed with a rigidity peculiar to those who are not at ease with set forms. There have always been Methodists who, like Wesley, loved the Anglican liturgy, but the importance of the Prayer Book in Methodism is that it was a background document, a standard of reference, a half-hidden but controlling norm. It was to this that Methodists turned for their liturgical requirements, and its phrases echoed in their extemporary prayers.

The ability to pray spontaneously was the hallmark of Methodist spirituality. Scholars are now aware that from New Testament times Christianity combined extemporary prayers with set forms and the modern charismatic movements have shown us again that the ability to address God from the heart is a real evidence of freedom of the spirit. There is a tradition of a Durham miner, who in his normal speech seemed capable of nothing but the broadest dialect, but when he began to pray immediately achieved a perfection of lyrical English. On the other hand, such prayer could sometimes be very much in the vernacular, witness this prayer for a new minister from Lancashire in the nineteenth century: 'Of Lord, give him th'eye o' the'eagle, so he con spy sin a long way off. Glue his honds to th' Gospil plough. Tee his tongue to th'line o' truth. Nail his ear to t' Gospil pow (pole). Bow his yed deawn between his knees and his knees deawn in some lonesome dark and narrow valley, wheer prayer is much wanted to be made. Anoint him wi' th' oil o' salvation and set him afire. Amen.'

The hymns of Charles Wesley were much more the staple diet of Methodist spirituality both public and private. It is doubtful if Anglicans have ever regarded *Hymns Ancient and Modern* as a help to private prayer, while it would probably not occur to Romans, who came to modern hymnology in the late nineteenth rather than the eighteenth century, to place the *Westminster Hymnal* on the same shelf as the *Simple Prayer Book*, or the *Garden of the Soul*. But many Methodists found a link between the Church service and their daily devotions by 'taking the hymn book into the secret place', as one of them somewhat pietistically put it. And this, as was so often reiterated in the early days of the ill fated Anglican-Methodist conversation, was a great bulwark of Catholic faith.

There is little point in pausing for long to illustrate this statement. It has been done often enough in the past fifty or sixty years, lastly and not least notably, in 1966, by two Anglicans, H. A. Hodges and A. M. Allchin. In *A Rapture of Praise* they divide their selection into *Hymns on the Christian Year* and *Hymns on the Christian Life*. The former includes three stanzas on Calvary:

> 'God of unexampled grace,
>   Redeemer of mankind,
> Matter of eternal praise
>   We in thy passion find; ...
>
> Endless scenes of wonder rise
> With that mysterious tree,

Crucified before our eyes
Where we our Maker see:

Jesus, Lord, what hast Thou done?
Publish we the death divine,
Stop, and gaze, and fall, and own
Was never love like thine!'

The latter this on holiness:

'Jesus, the First and Last,
On thee my soul is cast:
Thou didst thy work begin
By blotting out my sin;
Thou wilt the root remove,
And perfect me in love.

Yet when the work is done,
The work is but begun:
Partaker of thy grace,
I long to see thy face;
The first I prove below,
The last I die to know.'

There is nothing in the hymns which an orthodox Catholic could not approve and there is much, particularly in those on the Eucharist, which would astonish him; for instance:

'With solemn faith we offer up,
And spread before Thy glorious eyes,
That only ground of all our hope,
That previous, bleeding sacrifice,
Which brings Thy grace on sinners down,
And perfects all our souls in one.'

Wesley here drew from the *Christian Sacrament and Sacrifice* of Daniel Brevint, Chaplain to the wife of the great French Marshal, Turenne.

These hymns on the Lord's Supper affirm unequivocally the Real Presence of Christ in the sacrament, though with the familiar Anglican agnosticism as to its precise mode. There are hints of the Jewish belief that the act of remembrance made possible a miracle in time so that the worshipping people became the contemporaries of gospel events. It is this belief which allows Wesley to sing of the Eucharist as in some sense a sacrifice, for 'Thy offering is ever new'. The hymns also have an eschatalogical note, congenial to theologians today, in that they regard the sacrament as a pledge and foretaste of the life of the fully consummated kingdom of God.

But some of these hymns were not allowed to remain in the section for use at communion. They were scattered about the Wesleyan hymn books and even John Wesley himself assigned the verses on the Eucharistic sacrifice illustrated above to the section 'For Believers Seeking Full Redemption'.

If we want to describe the spirituality of the average Methodist member as distinct from the preacher, teacher, and theologian, we must think of the singing of the hymns rather than the words. Congregational singing was the characteristic feature of Methodist worship. It was often raucous, sometimes too ostentatious and in sorry violation of Wesley's own rules, which are strangely like what Bonhoeffer writes in *Life Together*. For instance: 'Sing modestly. Do not bawl, so as to be heard above or distinct from the rest of the congregation, that you may not destroy the harmony; but strive to unite your voices together, so as to make one clear melodious sound.'

The church became the place where one went for a good sing and a good sermon; perhaps above all, the place where you were warmly received, made welcome and recognized. Your name would be known, you might be asked to fill some office, if you were sick you would be visited.

The sermon dominated and still dominates Methodist worship. Most people judged it by its ability to interest and amuse, and for its homely advice rather than its theology. They remembered its anecdotes rather than its doctrines. It was also regarded by many as the solemn climax towards which all the action of the worship moved and unquestionably such people found inspiration and help for daily living in the 'message'. The preacher himself was empowered to order the worship and he would often regard it as the setting for the precious jewel of the sermon. This was what made the visit to church profitable or otherwise. People went to hear the preacher. And the Sunday preachers' names are still displayed outside the larger Methodist churches, though they are, for the most part, meaningless to passers-by.

The effect must not be disparaged; it was not political revolution as in Puritan times; it was often merely a vague sense of 'uplift' which resulted ('Thank you for a lovely message'), or sometimes that strangely comforting sense of discomfort which follows the denunciation of public and private evil as though castigation were the catharsis. But when all the deficiencies of education by the spoken word have been exposed, it is probably true that people learned more from a monologue by a charismatic personality—though that in most cases is very little—than from all the ploys of group dynamics or the mechanical aids of technology. The religious notions of middle-aged Methodists have been formed chiefly by preachers of the past and there is nothing in the church of today to replace them.

There is, and for the whole of the century always has been, a gulf between the official statements of the theologians, the foundation documents, the faith of the intelligentia, and the spirituality of the ordinary members of some urban or rural society. There Wesley might be less prominent than Sankey and it is still instructive to study the reports of Methodist services and meetings in the local press, where the soloist will sing 'How Great Thou Art' and 'Just For Today' and the address may be a simple exposition of the blessings which attend trust in God or a plea for more love and kindness in the world. There is nothing here to distinguish Methodism from the general culture of non-liturgical, crypto-revivalist Christianity.

The typical Methodist was essentially a decent man, though, now and then he was found out in crafty business manoeuvres or harsh dealings. The ideals, however, were kindliness, mutual aid, a warm friendliness and sobriety. The Methodist did not live ostentatiously or luxuriously. His social life was often bounded by the non-alcoholic suppers and concerts held on church premises. He ate plenty of bread with his ham and salad or pork pie and drank tea at all seasons and homemade lemon water in the summer. He would give generously to Home or Overseas Missions and work with zest for the good causes sponsored by his church which captured his imagination.

Sunday was divided almost entirely between home and church.

Worship twice was often the rule plus attendance at afternoon Sunday School either as a teacher or pupil. Evening services were best attended.

The church community was often rent by quarrels and jealousies. Those who expected acknowledgment and did not receive it were quick to take offence. Families or individuals often left churches on personal grounds and attached themselves elsewhere. Sometimes they quarrelled openly at church meetings. Older and younger could resent each other and argue bitterly about the allocation of rooms for their respective activities. But there were always some who could tell the story of their conversion or who pursued a quiet, faithful life of church loyalty and waiting on the ordinances of the Gospel. Regular worship, teaching at Sunday School or leadership of a group of members in a Society Class, the treasurership of some organization or other, plus a known Christian profession in daily work, positive in its very negatives of no swearing, drinking or enjoying lewd jokes, made up the rule of life for many. There were also some attempts to pray at home, sometimes in the family as well as alone. The decline of family prayers, largely owing to the embarrassment of the rising generation, gave a bad conscience to many of the Methodists before the Second World War. But Wesley's distinctive teaching that the believer should press on to perfect love was vague in the consciousness of the majority, a problem to the better informed and more thoughtful ministers, a 'grand depositum' only to theologians or to a few prophets of holiness. Methodism, of all movements, had come to lower the honours standard of Christian life and abolish the pass degree.

This pattern has been dislocated for many by social change. Three developments in particular have made the Methodist not only less the product of his original tradition, but have gone far to abolish the culture of the corner shop in which for about a hundred years he flourished.

One is the vast increase in university education. When Methodists were a small minority in the older universities they preserved a distinctive life and helped one another when drunkards soused their beds with water. Indeed, in spite of the large Methodist Societies which ecumenism and radicalism did not succeed in destroying in the 1960s, Methodists are not distinctive as such. Some of them may be adherents of the Christian Union, but if so it is their conservative evangelicalism which they share with Anglicans, Baptists and others, which distinguishes them, and not their Methodist membership. The rest will conform to the prevailing customs.

It is those Methodists whose university education was completed ten years ago and have become absorbed in the world of scholarship and big business who are little different to their contemporaries to outward view. They will come to the worship of their church perhaps on average once a fortnight. They will support its work financially and may even edit the church newsletter, or help in the Sunday School. They may be relied on for Christian Aid or National Children's Home collecting and they will maintain the semblance, and perhaps for more, of a united and happy family life. But they will drink wine at dinner parties and perhaps beer and even spirits occasionally at home. Nor will they necessarily avoid the wilder social occasions of their milieu, though they will be temperate in most things. What haunts some of them is their commitment to the present system; they benefit from the advantages of capitalism and work for firms with investments in South Africa. They are inexorably bound to the order of the affluent West, and though at times they feel guilty, they continue to run two cars if this seems expedient. The extent of their rebellion is that they may vote Labour rather than Conservative.

The notorious mobility of the population in our time is the second factor in the disintegration of Methodism; the constant movement from place to place and also the ease of which transfer from one social class to another may now be accomplished. This adversely affects a close knit movement such as Methodism which depends so much on personal friendship and the integration of individuals in the church community. Change itself encourages the weakening of religious ties, for although Methodism is 'connexion' and, in theory, has an advantage over other communions in that the Methodists in one place may easily be informed of the arrivals from another, it is all too easy for the migrants not to engage too closely in the church life of their new home. They may welcome the opportunity to escape from the imprisonment of the narrow world of their previous chapel; they may have decided that too much of their leisure was formerly given to church work; or they may be aliens in a subtly different style of Methodist, more formal, or more free. Traditional Methodism does demand a society of friends and where this is not found the raison d'être of church attendance seems lost. There is no Mass to make the worshipper—despite all alternative canons and the vernacular—quickly at home in Belgravia or Bolton.

There is, thirdly, the fact that intense evangelicalism always provokes its own reaction. A tutor at the Headingly Theological Institution (for ministerial training) in the 1850s said that Methodism had achieved more by *conquest* than by nurture. During the First World War, R. N. Flew, later an eminent theologian, deplored those of his contemporaries who 'tried to force every experience on to the procrustean bed of their own narrow holiness' and there was a group of Wesleyan theological teachers surrounding the Yorkshireman W. R. Maltby who felt that there was more of God in the world among worldly people than the revivalist preachers would ever admit. They wanted the poets' and novelists' vision of human life in its splendour and its pathos, to lighten evangelical despair and the Christ of Galilee to liberate his followers from the bloodless categories of a scholastic Paulinism much as they loved the author of Romans 8.

Through the 1920s and 1930s there was a gradual liberation. Theatres were no longer proscribed as of the devil. Dramatic and Music societies were permitted and at last, in 1942, dancing and card games were allowed on Methodist premises. In 1974 the Methodist Conference ceased to urge Methodist members to become total abstainers and left the matter to responsible personal decision. There was less preaching for sudden conversion; more guidance about the problems of Christian life in the world, suffering and war, and personal relationships. Leslie Weatherhead, for instance, concentrated many of his great gifts on presenting a view of God which realistic, thoughtful people would accept, on helping them to understand themselves better and on teaching them meditation. In more recent years the lesson has been well learned that Christianity involves political understanding and social responsibility. Few Methodists are now ignorant of the need to bring aid to the underdeveloped nations and to relieve the distress of the hungry, the homeless, and the victims of natural disasters and war.

But a price has been paid. The old simplicities are gone, perhaps never to return, except in the conservative evangelicalism which is not truly Methodist, or occasional corybanticism, which is atavistic and not likely to flourish in the modern tightly organized and emotionally sane if rather dull companies of the Methodist people.

The Charismatic Movement has its Methodist students and devotees; but the spiritual descendants of John Wesley are not in the van of this movement. Some individuals have found great liberation through the charismatic gifts but there has been no fire sweeping the connexion.

There has been an increase in sacramental observances and in teaching about churchmanship. The Lord's Supper is administered at least once a month in the larger churches, probably twice or three times in most of them, and many people are glad of this else it would not have happened. A new Methodist Eucharist has been constructed with the old title of Wesley's own adaptation of the Book of Common Prayer, *The Sunday Service*. This is based on those principles of the liturgical tradition which all churches now recognize—the unity of Word and Sacrament and the fourfold shape of the Supper—he took (offertory and the setting of the table), he gave thanks (canon or anaphora, or great prayer with anamnesis), he broke (fraction or breaking of the bread), he gave to them (distribution or sharing of bread and wine). If Methodist preachers come to understand the technique of the liturgical sermon, the Methodist gift of preaching could possibly revive the art for the benefit of all the churches. By 'the liturgical sermon' I understand the succinct exposition of one of the prescribed passages —or indeed of some insight common to them all—and its application both to the lives of the hearers and to the holy mystery in which they are joined.

The revised *Sunday Service* unashamedly addresses God in the second person plural whereas its predecessor provided alternative columns, one in the 'Thou' form, the other in 'You'. It also uses the new ecumenical translations of common texts—*Gloria in Excelsis*, *Lord's Prayer* and *Nicene Creed*. The traditional Methodist order, received from Wesley, which is primarily the rite of the 1662 *Book of Common Prayer* will appear in the new *Methodist Service Book*; it is worth knowing that in its eucharistic revisions, Methodism has acted independently of the Church of England, though it has availed itself of the lectionary of the Joint Liturgical

Group to which all the major British groups now send representatives.

In the post-war years there has been great stress on teaching and elaborate programmes have been devised. To some extent the educationalists have captured the mind of the church, and worship has not been sufficiently understood in its own right but seen too much as a part of 'training'. Candidates for church membership or confirmation as the more exact Catholic term now has it, are now carefully prepared, but this is no guarantee of their fidelity or inevitable safeguard against disenchantment, and the denomination as a whole continues to decline.

This, however, is the culmination of a long process which began not with the union of Wesleyan, Primitive and United Methodists in 1932 or with the shock of the 1914 war, but at least a century ago when the increase in Methodists no longer kept pace with the increase in population.

Methodists have shown themselves as singularly open as their founder to developments outside their borders. The Iona and Taizé communities have their Methodist disciples and there has been more than a slight stirring in recent years of a desire for a renewed discipline and life of prayer achieved through groups binding themselves together in a common life. Some would even seek to found orders within Methodism. There is a proper restlessness and discontent with the present state of the church and a desire, the product of great humility, and devoid of arrogance, for a more apostolic life. Methodism may always be parasitic upon older communions and traditions which were ancient in its infancy; it may not be the form of Christianity in which men of genius—the Chestertons, Eliots, Audens and Waughs—find their home, but it could still retain and recover the spirit of a family of faith, without exaggerated enthusiasm or fanatical pride, 'humble and teachable and mild', but resolute in its waiting for the Kingdom of God and Catholic in its love.

5

DISSENT AND DESCENT

Brian Frost and Leo Pyle

Dissent and Descent

LEO PYLE AND BRIAN FROST

CATHOLICISM—a rigid body coming to life? Methodism —a prophetic movement of the Spirit hardening and decaying? Is this a true picture of these two Churches in Britain at the present time? Although many scholars would question whether Methodists have ever been part of historic dissent in the same way as have Baptists, Quakers and Congregationalists, early Methodists' awareness of the Holy Spirit can surely not be denied. As Methodism has become institutionalized there have always been people to recall the charismatic quality of early Methodism.

However, Methodism has never been able to forget its Anglican roots even in its eagerness to follow the promptings of the Holy Spirit. And modern Methodism seems to imply that despite the failure of one union scheme it is being led into a new relationship with Anglicanism by the same Spirit. This can be seen as the Methodist community seeking after descent and historic continuity. It may mean the end of Methodism as a dissenting body and this is perhaps why those who see themselves in the prophetic tradition are most afraid of any merger.

Paradoxically the Scarlet Woman—the phrase so often used of the Church of Rome by many in the prophetic tradition—seems herself to be moving away from the rigid, ordered, structured monolith of history to a free, disorderly, argumentative society of friends.

It has taken English Catholics over a hundred years to begin to escape from the Roman outlook and structure which were considerably augmented by the restoration of the Catholic Hierarchy in 1850. Though this implied a formal acceptance of Catholicism in Britain Catholics viewed it as the first step towards the restoration of the true, Roman faith. Today the signs of tension among English Catholics point to what has already happened in Holland—the emergence of a genuine national Church. An attempt to quench it is being made by the cautious, juridicial, prudent Roman mind.

It is surely therefore very appropriate that these two Churches should continue to explore with each other as these essays have tried to the relationship between the two traditions which can be summed up by the two words 'Dissent' and 'Descent', seeking to discover an authentic relationship between prophet and priest, spirit and order, past, present and future.

The essays have tried to examine the forces in the two traditions creating these tensions and how they have arisen. Is the church for example but the innocent victim of a society now feeling the full impact of mobility and secularism without any dynamism of its own?

For Methodism, Wesley's adage 'Get all you can, save all you can, give all you can' certainly encouraged the growth of a prosperous middle class. Some historians, as Lampard (pp. 25–6) makes clear, have gone so far as to assert that this prevented a revolution in England similar to the French Revolution in the late eighteenth century. Others have seen this assessment as one of the fantasy pictures of the religious mind and its messianic projections.

What cannot be doubted is that Methodism's schizophrenia in the nineteenth century—the High Toryism of the Wesleyans and the articulate radicalism of the Primitive Methodists—has now been absorbed into the liberalism of the do-gooders. Who would now remember that Methodists were deeply involved with the creation of the Agricultural Worker's Union? Even though one leader of the Labour Party considered that it owed more to Methodism than Marx, in a sense Methodism is now the church of Victorian irrelevance. Thirty or so Methodist M.P.s may testify to this. It was not this group in the 1960s which stood up and protested against Labour Government policy during the service in a Methodist church in Brighton at the time of annual Labour Party Conference.

Catholicism has a different past to live down. In the nineteenth century the High Toryism of the old Catholic families like the Norfolks, who had helped to preserve the Catholic Faith in England since the time of the Reformation, dominated and dictated to the large, Irish working class who made up the majority of the laity. There was no articulate radicalism; this group, urban and semiliterate, may very well have been as radical as the Primitive Methodists but it never said so.

In the first half of the twentieth century to this state of affairs was added the articulate romantic medieval view of the Church's role in society so well expressed, for example, by G. K. Chesterton. For him the Church ought to be the centre and focal point of society and its culture.

Now this view is being challenged. Catholicism in Britain is undergoing profound changes due to the rise of a Catholic middle class, benefiting from the increased educational opportunities created by the 1944 Education Act. The new-found vitality of the laity comes from this group of people. Will they follow in the wake of the liberalism of the do-gooders as they take their grammar-school ideals on to the playing fields of Westminster or is it too early yet to see their impact on the Church?

Certainly these ideals are bound to represent a challenge to the dominant idea as expressed in countless pastoral letters: *plus ça change, plus c'est la même chose.* They will not be helped by those converts to Catholicism who have been drawn by the appeal of solidity, authoritarianism and a sense of historic continuity to bring the education, ideas and vitality that the old families had never been able to provide. It is ironic that it is this very group which is now itself threatened by change.

These tensions are in striking contrast to Methodism where conversion has often been an hysterical rather than an historical phenomenon. Some indeed would say that the numerical decline and fall of Methodism is related to the loss of the hysterical and the recovery of the historical. And there are those in Catholicism who would see its recovery as the ultimate threat to both the mission and commission of the body of Christ. For such Catholics numbers count: Catholicism is a success story when its sales equal those of the *Daily Express*: Methodism is a failure when its sales are only those of the *Guardian*. Other Catholics, however, would see the emergence of intelligent, committed and free-thinking laity as the point of creative change. For them change is a friend.

Welcoming the decline and fall of the prophet and priest in the two traditions (where neither the pulpit nor the altar are dominated by the preacher and the celebrant), as worship becomes the work of the whole community so they see the mission of the church in terms of lay people coming together to worship and then being dispersed in the world. Living in a mobile world they know the need to be free from an obsession with buildings and with the Church as an institution so that they may be liberated to be the people of God on the move.

This is not to say that the so-called 'non-conformist' conscience (drink and gambling have never been the milk and honey of Christ's people) or the cohesive group loyalty and stubbornness of the Catholic ghetto have not helped to bring us to the present situation. Indeed, Cardinal Manning's intervention in the dock strike at the end of the nineteenth century and Hugh Price Hughes' preaching about social righteousness at the beginning of the twentieth were themselves symbols of changing attitudes.

The most significant point of their response was the attempt to come to terms with a society undergoing changes through industrialization and urbanization. But this pattern has now accelerated with the rise of the modern city and the mobile patterns of work and life. The gathering of the people in central hall for uplift and the gathering round the altar for sanctification must now give way to eucharistic politics where the shared bread of the Eucharist is identified with the bread of the world. Christian concern for the problems of world hunger starts and ends here. But it is more than that—the bread which we break each Eucharist points us to Christ broken in the world.

People are being uprooted from the traditional northern citadels of the Methodist and Catholic Salvation Armies and brought south to the city. Through leaders like Archbishop Roberts and Lord Soper a mobile God has been bridging the gaps between the puritanical milieu of the north and the cosmopolitanism of the south, pointing to a church which relates to the rise of the meritocracy. But one Donald Soper does not make a Methodist summer nor one Archbishop Roberts a Catholic spring.

It is here—in an urban world where even rural communities depend utterly on the city—that a contemporary ministry needs working out by the laity in dispersal as it learns to overcome its obsession with its pulpit and altar father figures. But how can the church of the city ever learn to throw off not only its father figures but its rural blinkers? Can it ever learn from the mistakes rather than the successes of its past? Are Methodists right to look more upon the Church as an institution created by Christ, stemming the ages and continents, and Catholics to seek the body of Christ as local, national, indigenous and diverse? If this happens how will this affect the love-hate relationship which exists between both groups and the Church of England?

Perhaps the new friendship of Methodists and Catholics in Britain covers up an unspoken doctrine: 'Methodists and Catholics of England unite, you have only the Church of England to fear.' Yet it is perhaps as difficult for Catholics to lose their feelings of superiority over the Church of England as for Methodists to lose their inferiority complexes; these two group phenomena are bound to bedevil relationship as the churches come to grips with their mission. For urban mission cannot be seen in terms of Catholics and Methodists understanding each other but in all Christians in their dispersion participating in Christ's ministry to the whole of the city.

We do not yet know what a suitable structure for this ministry looks like nor if it will make any difference. Some, by rejecting the structures of the Roman Church completely and others with a concept of non-Church have already given their answer with their feet. Is it only the sense of historical continuity which prevents other Christians following in their footsteps?

Will even the dated non-Church idea itself harden and become rigid if it succeeds? Both the rise of the Church of England at the Reformation in the sixteenth century and the rise of Methodism from the Church of England in the latter half of the eighteenth century were the emergence of new life. However, the institutions created by this new life have themselves stifled it and given rise to the frustrated radicalism of those who in turn wish to transform the established order.

This hardening and frustration which continually recurs in Church history is because Christians have not seen the Church as the people of God continually on the move through history, re-constituted by the coming of the Spirit at Pentecost and expecting the consummation of all things and all people at the end of time. As these chapters have indicated Pentecost, far from being the preoccupation of a lunatic fringe, is the renewing of the church for sharing in Christ's redemption of the world. What does this redemption imply? Certainly there is a proper relationship between spirit and structure, priest and prophet. If Catholics in the past have identified spirit with hierarchic structure and Methodists scorned the Spirit's

97

involvement with structure, both now need to learn the essentially dialogical nature of the Spirit's work. Then the Church becomes that part of the world where Christ is seen, worshipped and witnessed to.

But Christ is not identified with the Church—for he is head of the new creation. He both loves and judges it. If Methodists cannot tolerate the love of Christ for his erring Church, Catholics seem unable to accept his judgement. Both alike seem to need a new dialectic between spirit and structure, love and hate.

Where then do we look for the New Jerusalem? Certainly not in the wrong relationships generated by both Methodist and Catholic authoritarian patterns in the local and national church, in the district and the diocese, however excellent these may once have been. For this produces not only truncated relationships within the church but a stunted relationship between Church and society. W. B. Pope, J. H. Newman, Jabez Bunting, Cardinal Hinsley are revered father figures but what is surely urgently needed is an authentic lay theology which neither tradition has been able to produce, despite Methodism's vaunted lay initiatives in the realm of practical action and Catholicism's often brilliant minds like Belloc's and von Hugel's.

What would an authentic lay theology comprise? How could the clergy of both traditions learn to liberate their people for ministry? Part of the answer must surely lie in integrating theological college and university, theology and psychology, theology and sociology, theology and politics. Here the experience of the layman needs fertilising with the thinking of the theologian. This has transparently not happened in Methodism despite its genuine lay insights. It has also not happened in Catholicism because of the absence of articulate laymen in the world.

Is one problem simply that Methodism has been a movement in search of a theology and Catholicism a theology in search of a movement? The answer will surely be found more in a local situation of town or conurbation where all have a part to play than in a centralized authoritarian solution, but perhaps neither Church can stand the strain of an articulate laity, concerned for a ministry in an urban world. The tottering structure of both might collapse under such new pressures.

Such a lay theology of power must start from the idea of mission as the disclosure of Christ in all his roles. Too often in the past lay people have only been encouraged to see Jesus in a few of his roles—as saviour, judge, victim. When only a few of his roles are seen their very significance and meaning is perverted.

But in the New Testament Jesus plays many roles, not all as important as one another but all to be reckoned with. When Jesus is talked about as Lord and King he is shown as creator and sustainer of all things and all men. He has therefore no need of us to take him to the world—he is already present, reigning through the cross by which all history was transformed. All we have to do is make this fact present and visible.

So Christian group life with its concern for buildings, its desire for 'Christian' fellowship, its sacramentalism suitably isolated so that the Eucharist is the most holy instead of the most secular moment of the week, serves not to equip the people of God but to edify egos already closed to Christ's presence in the world. For in this kind of Church mission is seen as the bringing of the world to the holy place.

The true pattern of Christian group life is to be found where Christians are as hidden in the world as Christ became in the Incarnation. Surely this must mean the end of 'Christian' groups and Christian pressure groups? For Christ is already related to all groups, and they are under his reign when they are actively working for the transformation of man in society.

In view of this can we dare to assume that the present patterns of citizenship for both traditions are political enough? Has the politics of the pressure group been thought out other than in opposition to the abortion and divorce bills and alarm at the millions spent on gambling with an occasional touch of anxiety over the armaments race? Perhaps these groups have only existed to make the Church respectable as an apology for a genuine cutting edge. Surely supremely in our time Christians must be found in the less personal forms of group life which have grown up in urban society to cater for the complicated structures we need. They must also be found in groups trying to change the patterns of aid and trade across the world. For it is insufficient to wish to preserve 'little England' when we live on the strength of world poverty. It is here that we must learn to see and respond to Christ as Lord of creation, not only Lord of Europe!

But we are to learn to see him too as Son of Man, as man with man, as the chapter on Mission has pointed out. It is through Christ that man learns to come of age. Man's striving to be fully human must therefore receive the encouragement and affirmation of Christians. 'Applied Christianity'—whether of the Catholic desire to sanctify what is thought to be not holy outside the church, or the Methodist desire to redeem the fallen environment—are both denials of the Son of Man. They must be supplemented by a Christ who progressively humanizes the power groups and the culture of a society. In the past the Christian has often been preoccupied with prohibition for man—both of pill and pub—with a strong tendency to build a social security system for Christians. None would deny the need for voluntary organizations: but we must emphasize continually that Jesus was not a Christian.

Man's work is the crucial area where this is to be worked out. If Jesus as Son of Man can have no relationsip with a man's work what is wrong? And how can it be changed? Are Christians, moreover, sufficiently concerned with the factors in work which are de-humanizing? They must continually watch the environment in which men are called to work and the conditions of man's work, as well as the products, asking if the goods in an affluent society are justifiable in a world of acute poverty.

However there is a danger of a new puritanism in this approach which can only be avoided by seeing the inter-relationship of the personal and the social. Only when the Eucharist is seen as the one bread for the world, made for man, by man, offered by the Man, will the things of this world be the things of Christ. And the personal and the political properly related.

Until the time when Christ will sum up all history, Christ's mission in the world where he has established the Church will be a continuation of the acceptance and judgement disclosed by his death and resurrection. But it will be a long time before we learn the Pentecostal truth that Christ is the missionary!

In Catholic circles it has been through recognizing the presence of Christ and his role in the world that he has been found anew in the bread and wine. In that sense the world has been the starting place for a recovery of Christ's real presence in the worshipping community.

Yet both the Methodist and Catholic traditions have looked upon the Eurcharist as a pious and religious exercise for individual and community, although in Methodism there have been many content to regard Eucharistic faith and practice as an optional extra trammelling the free course of the Spirit. Though the Catholic Eucharist in the past has seemed essentially corporate, in fact it has encouraged the growth of a pious individualism unrelated to other worshippers and unrelated to the world.

Any talk of the secular nature of the eucharist is bound to leave both communities startled and apprehensive. Whether either of these communities can ever realize the truly secular nature of the eucharist—the meaning of Christ's real presence—is an open question. Can they ever do so without political awareness? How can both traditions be freed from their obsessive individualism without lapsing into a corporateness equally divorced from the world, as where Catholic sacramentalism is concerned only with the minutiae of the liturgy? This is the crucial question for a secular Eucharist: 'There is no holiness without social holiness' (Wesley). Both traditions seem to be struggling to rediscover the centrality of the Eucharist. Paradoxically, Catholics have often thought that their understanding, based as it is on recent Biblical scholarship, was bringing them closer to the Protestant tradition, yet for many Methodists the new language now being used about the Eucharist would seem hardly commendable or correct.

The dangers inherent in attempting to combine form and spirit, liturgy and spontaneity, will be obvious to Methodists, who have often suffered and endured so-called prophetic prayer, which has lost its freshness. In this form of prayer spirit and structure have lost their interrelationship and a new kind of liturgical preoccupation with content has taken the place of what is authentic in the prophetic tradition.

In the end what matters is whether our reflection upon the world and our awareness of it makes us sensitive to what we have learnt and the Christ we have met. Then we will have learnt to meet him there in order to meet him everywhere.

In order to meet him everywhere we need to rediscover the breaking of the Word. Preaching must now surely stem from a group of lay people (including the preacher!) wrestling with their problems in everyday life, and reflecting on them in the light of Biblical insights. Then local people may feel that their concerns and the preaching of the Word have a real relationship to one another.

Are groups such as we know them, in particular the structures of the local churches, sufficient or appropriate to understand these truths and live them out? Is the church any longer the right place for the Eurcharist? How can the rigid behaviour patterns of both traditions, organized as they are so firmly and securely, ever do this without a radical transformation or disintegration? These are unanswered questions these essays raise. Such a departure will start with baptism as the ordination of the People of God for participation in Christ's worldly mission. Baptism, then, far from being a religious act, becomes an action turned to the world, and a reminder of God's loving concern for all life: it is the most revolutionary act in which a Christian can be involved.

Worship then begins to relate to the mission of humanizing and healing the world. Hitherto spirituality has been very much related to the sacred cows of the two Churches: hymn-singing and veneration of the saints, together with the mediation of Christ's life through individual confession and the class meeting. Now, however, Christ's priestly role implies a far greater understanding and dependence on group work and the tensions and problems of our own power drives and needs. Do we need to act out in worship our aggressions and conflicts, perhaps through mime and dialogue? Do we need to involve doctors, social workers and psychiatrists as well as the many natural intuitives often at work unobtrusively in our midst?

These tensions are, of course, part of more complex ones in the contemporary world where immense technical skill co-exists with acute misery, a curiosity about the environment does not prevent its despoilation. Moreover, the new apparent closeness of nations and groups through travel, TV and radio, brings with it a recoil from the clash of cultures such proximity generates.

Christians, as others, are caught in these changes and radically affected by them. Any dynamic response they can give will come only from a new theology drawn from experience of these tensions. However, some in both traditions are terrified of theology, the Methodist often preferring to rely on the Spirit, the Catholic on the given structure.

But underneath the given structures new patterns of worship

and belief seem to be emerging: in Catholicism in the direction of more variety; in Methodism, a movement towards uniformity. It remains difficult, nevertheless, adequately to reflect in action and thought the local and global tensions so bafflingly diverse and interconnected.

Within Catholicism there can be little growth in this direction unless more diversity of approach is allowed, but there will be many opponents of a change to a theology of church and society which takes what has been described as 'the global village' more seriously.

In Methodism the implications of a movement towards a more Anglican view of church and state, and a willingness to look at what Catholics and Methodists have in common, will call for a greater catholicity and a more sophisticated critique of culture. In both cases previous attitudes must be rejected. For both Churches such a re-appraisal will not be without fear and flight into the past. This could lead either to breaking-point or to a new form of Christ in the world.

Much will depend on the wisdom of the personalities and pressure groups which exist in both bodies. Catholicism, seeking to establish itself through conformity even though in Britain doctrinally it has seemed non-conformist, hates the prophet. As a result any group or individual can be exposed to unfair charges of disloyalty if they try to force changes or point to global movements within the Roman Catholic Church.

Methodists, despite prophetic origins, and strong tendencies to innovation, are ambivalent about those who doubt and question. They, too, are open to the same charges of disloyalty and a lack of trust in the Gospel's reconciling work.

We know from history that often the tension between descent —a love for the past and a conservation of its good aspects—and dissent—a desire for change and a willingness to create new forms and institutions—has been the creative point leading to new life. But always the same question poses itself: can any institution tolerate the prophetic?

Could either Methodism or Catholicism welcome and survive a cultural revolution in attitudes, styles, organization and understanding of mission? Yet without such changes they can hardly survive, despite the fact that groups can perpetuate themselves long after the vision sustaining them has atrophied.

The irony behind both bodies is surely this: a Christian is committed to a doctrine of change which implies a movement towards a future which is always being renewed. Hope for such a Christian is central, not peripheral, to his existence: the past is always becoming contemporary and pointing to what is yet to be. Certainly scholars in both traditions agree such a doctrine is the nerve centre of the eschatology of the New Testament. But do the churches?

We must hope, with one eye on the past, Methodists and Catholics can be freed from its burden, able to learn its lessons, and be available together for the future.

APPENDIX A

Questions for discussion

1 CHURCH AND SOCIETY

1 To which social groups do Methodists and Catholics belong in your area?
2 What effect does a secular society like Britain have on minority Christian groups?
3 What role do people like Pope John XXIII play in helping society and the Church to begin to understand one another more fully?
4 Can you see a resemblance between political attitudes and the type of Christian community to which you belong?

2 THE CHURCH

1 How far are members of the Methodist and Catholic communities in Britain 'dissenters'?
2 Are there marks of 'Pentecostalism' in both Catholicism and Methodism?
3 How do changes in world society affect changes going on in the Methodist and Catholic Churches?
4 Is Methodism a religious order?

3 MISSION

1 In what ways ought the mission of the Church to be 'subversive'?
2 What does the Bible teach about 'religion' as it is referred to in this chapter?
3 Does being a pilgrim church mean first doing theology, then applying the results in action, or vice versa?

4 How is the tension between Christ as Son of God and Christ as Son of Man reflected in your local church or community situation?

4 WORSHIP AND SPIRITUALITY

1 Discuss the relative importance in the two traditions of hymns, sermons and liturgical actions in the light of your own personal experience.
2 Take a book of Roman Catholic and Methodist spirituality, read them together, and discuss your reactions and reflections.
3 Go together to a Methodist and Catholic act of worship and share your reactions in the group.
4 Discuss your responses to two hymns which you have selected from a Methodist and a Catholic hymn book.

APPENDIX B

Books for further reading

1 CHURCH AND SOCIETY

E. P. Thompson, *The Making of the English Working Class* (Penguin).
Bernard Semmel, *The Methodist Revolution* (Heinemann).
Bryan Wilson, *Religion in Secular Society* (Penguin).
Rupert E. Davies, *Methodism* (Penguin).
David Martin, *The Sociology of Religion* (SCM).
D. Matthew, *Catholicism in England, 1535-1935* (Longmans 1936).

2 THE CHURCH

John Todd, *John Wesley and the Catholic Church* (Catholic Book Club).
R. A. Markus, *Saeculum—History and Society in the Theology of St Augustine* (Cambridge University Press).
E. Schillebeeckx, *Christ the Sacrament* (Sheed and Ward).

3 MISSION

Pauline Webb, *Are We Yet Alive?* (Epworth).
Pauline Webb, *Salvation Today* (SCM).
Colin Morris, *Mankind my Church* (Hodder and Stoughton).
Living Parish Pamphlets (Ealing Abbey, Charlbury Grove, W5).

4 WORSHIP AND SPIRITUALITY

Oliver and Ianthe Pratt, *Let Liturgy Live* (Sheed and Ward).

J. Neville Ward, *The Use of Praying* (Epworth).
Gordon S. Wakefield, *Methodist Devotion* (Epworth).
H. A. Hodges and A. M. Allchin, *A Rapture of Praise* (SPCK).

5 DISSENT AND DESCENT

Webb, Sansbury, Slack, *Agenda for the Churches* (SCM).
Malcolm Sweeting, *Group Life in the Church* (Clinical Theology Association).
Reports of the Uppsala/Nairobi Assemblies of the World Council of Churches.

Three Papal encyclicals, *Pacem in Terris* (Peace on Earth), *Mater et Magistra*, and On the Development of Peoples, should also be consulted.

Also of interest is the Lutheran/Roman Catholic Dialogue on Papal Primacy, issued by the officially appointed Lutheran-Catholic Dialogue Group for the United States on 4th March, 1974, and *Catholics and Methodists*: An Introduction to the work of the Joint Commission between the World Methodist Council and the Roman Catholic Church since 1967 by R. L. Stewart (Catholic Truth Society, 1974).

The books in this appendix can be obtained (if still in print) from:

Lumen Books Ltd
    375 Lordship Lane
    London SE12

or from a local library.

APPENDIX C

Notes on Contributors

Father JOHN COVENTRY, S.J., born in 1915, and educated at Stony-hurst College, Heythrop College and Campion Hall, Oxford, was Headmaster of Beaumont College and later Provincial Superior of the English Jesuits. He was the first Secretary of the Roman Catholic National Ecumenical Commission when it was started in 1967, and remains a member of it.

BRIAN G. FROST, a Methodist layman since 1956 (though brought up in the Church of England), read English at Oxford University after two years' National Service as a private in the RAMC. At Oxford he was secretary of the Student Christian Movement, which confirmed his intention to serve the ecumenical movement. In 1960 he joined the staff of the Christian Aid Department of the British Council of Churches, leaving it in 1968 to become Programme Director of an Ecumenical Centre in Notting Hill (now located at St James's, Picadilly). His interest in new forms of worship led him (with the Rev. Derek Wensley) to edit two series of books containing new material, *Celebration* and *Tension*. He is also editor of *The Secular in the Sacred* (on the multi-purpose use of church buildings), The Tactics of Pressure, and a book of cartoons (with the Rev. Philip Spence) *Pardon My Prejudice*. All are published by Galliard.

CECILY HASTINGS has been a Roman Catholic since her birth in 1924 and a Marxist socialist for some years. Amongst the various ways in which she has made a living has been a good deal of translation, mainly theology and mostly from German (Hans Kung and Karl Rahner). This has been one main source of her theological education, another being more than fifteen years in the Catholic Evidence Guild, talking theology to non-specialists from platforms in Hyde Park and similar places. During the past nine years she has been in the Religious Studies Department of St Mary's College of Education, Strawberry Hill, Twickenham.

The Rev. JOHN S. LAMPARD is a Methodist Minister, working in Leeds. After qualifying as a solicitor he entered the Methodist ministry, studying at Bristol and Oklahoma, U.S.A. and obtaining degrees in theology and sociology, and the sociology of religion. He is active in the study of group dynamics and is Convenor of the Methodist Group Sensitivity Training Unit. His hobbies are commemorative pottery and reading. Married with two young children, he claims that his family have taught him more about group dynamics than any text-book.

MONICA MARY LAWLOR is a Roman Catholic, who has an Honours B.A. and a Ph.D. in psychology from the University of London. She is at present Senior Lecturer in Psychology at Bedford College, University of London. The main areas of psychology in which she is involved in teaching and research are child psychology, comparative psychology and the psychology of religion. She is a member of the Newman Association of which she has been a member of Council and the Honorary Secretary. Other interests are the study of theology, painting and gardening. She has written *Personal Responsibility* (1963), *Out of this World: a study of Catholic Values* (1965) and, with Simon Clements, *The McCabe Affair*, as well as articles in professional journals and religious periodicals.

Dr D. LEO PYLE was one of the founders of the Roman Catholic magazine *Slant*. He is a Cambridge graduate, married, with four children. He lectures in Chemical Engineering at Imperial College. He is joint editor with his wife of a book on *The Pill* (documentary reactions to Roman Catholic teaching on birth control). Actively concerned with issues of development, he has lectured in Santiago, Chile, during the Allende period, and in Canada, and has recently returned from Pakistan where he has been helping to assess development needs.

The Rev. TREVOR ROWE, B.Sc., M.A., B.D., is a Methodist Minister now lecturing in pastoral theology at The Queen's College, Birmingham, where he is responsible for developing pastoral studies as an integral part of theological education. For two years he was Chairman of The Board of Lay Training of the Methodist Church. Currently he is Chairman of 'All Faiths for One Race' in Birmingham. He is author of *St Augustine—Pastoral Theologian* (Epworth), the Fernley-Hartley Lecture for 1974.

JOHN M. TODD is the author of *Reformation, Martin Luther, John Wesley and The Catholic Church,* and a number of other books. He is also a publisher working with Darton, Longman & Todd Ltd. Born an Anglican, he was an agnostic for some time before becoming a Roman Catholic in 1944, along with other members of a pacifist land commune. He is active in the ecumenical movement, also in an adult education movement, *Catholic People's Weeks;* he is a Governor of a residential Centre for study and renewal in North Somerset—Ammerdown, near Radstock, Bath.

The Rev. GORDON S. WAKEFIELD is Chairman of the Manchester and Stockport District of the Methodist Church. From 1963–72 he was Connexional Editor and responsible for the publications of the Epworth Press. He is Chairman of the British Council of Churches' Committee for Unity in Prayer, a member of the Joint Liturgical Group, was on the 'Talks about Talks', and is co-editor with A. Raymond George of the forthcoming Methodist Service Book. His main interests apart from ecumenical activities, Church history and spirituality, are preaching, writing and cricket. His books include *Puritan Devotion, Methodist Devotion, The Life of the Spirit in the World of Today* and *Robert Newton Flew.*

PAULINE MARY WEBB, B.A., A.K.C., S.T.M., the daughter of a Methodist minister, began her career as a teacher. In 1954 she became Editor for the Methodist Missionary Society and in 1967 was appointed to a new and experimental post as Director of The Board of Lay Training of the Methodist Church, returning to the MMS in 1973 as Area Secretary for the Autonomous Churches in Africa and the Caribbean. An accredited lay preacher since 1953, Pauline Webb was elected Vice-President of the Methodist Conference in 1965. She is the author of a number of books, the most recent being *Salvation Today.* Her special interests include the ministry of the laity, race relations, the role of women in Church and community and the ecumenical movement. She represents Methodism on several inter-Church committees and is Vice-Chairman of the Central Committee of the World Council of Churches.